A Verse by Verse Trip Through
The Holy Land

Rob and Lisa Laizure

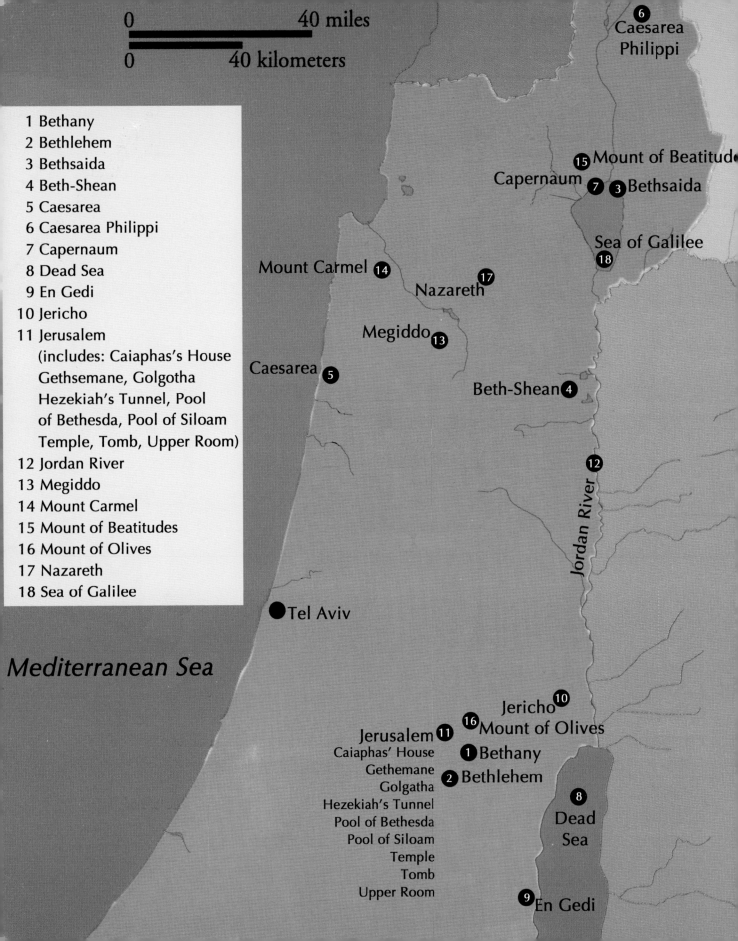

Scale:
0 — 40 miles
0 — 40 kilometers

Caesarea Philippi 6

Mount of Beatitude 15

Capernaum 7   3 Bethsaida

Sea of Galilee
18

Mount Carmel 14

Nazareth 17

Megiddo 13

Caesarea 5

Beth-Shean 4

Jordan River 12

Jericho 10

Mount of Olives 16

Jerusalem 11

Caiaphas' House   1 Bethany
Gethemane   2 Bethlehem
Golgatha
Hezekiah's Tunnel
Pool of Bethesda
Pool of Siloam
Temple
Tomb
Upper Room

Tel Aviv

Mediterranean Sea

Dead
Sea 8

9 En Gedi

Table of Contents

Welcome to the Holy Land! We hope your experience in this beautiful, historical land will touch your lives as much as it has touched ours. You will be viewing many sites in a short amount of time. It is sometimes difficult to put together what you are seeing with actual Biblical accounts. Our goal in putting this together is to help you connect the places in the Bible with actual verses in the Bible. As you do, we hope your faith will grow as you see the Bible come alive. If you are reading this without being in the Holy Land we hope this picture and verse tour will help you see the places where Abraham, David, Paul and Jesus walked. Our desire is to see your faith strengthened by viewing real places in this world that are attached to the Bible.

A brief historical overview will help you as you begin to put the pieces together of this incredible area that God gave his people. This is a very short account of thousands of years of history. In order to understand the land you will be seeing, we thought it might be helpful to know a little about Israel and why the places you will see are crucial pieces to our Christian faith.

And it all starts with Adam and Eve...

History begins with Adam and Eve in the Garden of Eden, which is most likely in modern day Iraq. **Genesis 2:10-14 says: Now a river flowed out of Eden to water the garden; and from there it divided and became four rivers. The name of the first is Pishon; it flows around the whole land of Havilah, where there is gold. The gold of that land is good; the bdellium and the onyx stone are there. The name of the second river is Gihon; it flows around the whole land of Cush. The name of the third river is Tigris; it flows east of Assyria. And the fourth river is the Euphrates.**

God created a beautiful, sin-free world until Adam and Eve sinned in the Garden of Eden. They were banished away from the peaceful, beautiful environment God created for them and forced to work the ground in hardship and bear children in pain. Through their descendants, the world became a god-less society that was eventually destroyed by the flood in the time of Noah. Through the children of Noah, the world eventually became populated again and Abram (or Abraham) showed up on the scene hundreds of years later. He was living in Ur, which is our modern day Iraq. God called him to leave his home and go to a new land, the land of Canaan or the Promised Land which is now modern day Israel.

Genesis 12:1-7: Now the Lord said to Abram, "Go forth from your country, and from your relatives and from your father's house, to the land which I will show you; and I will make you a great nation, and I will bless you, and make your name great; and so you shall be a blessing; and I will bless those who bless you, and the one who curses you I will curse. And in you all the families of the earth will be blessed." So Abram went forth as the Lord had spoken to him; and Lot went with him. Now Abram was seventy-five years old when he departed from Haran. Abram took Sarai his wife and Lot his nephew, and all their possessions which they had accumulated, and the persons which they had acquired in Haran, and they set out for the land of Canaan; thus they came to the land of Canaan. Abram passed through the land as far as the site of Shechem, to the oak of Moreh. Now the Canaanite was then in the land. The Lord appeared to Abram and said, "To your descendants I will give this land." So he built an altar there to the Lord who had appeared to him.

Abraham had a son Isaac who had a son Jacob. Jacob had twelve sons which the Bible refers to as the patriarchs of the Twelve Tribes of Israel. Each son was allotted a certain portion of the land in Israel. Jacob's 11th son Joseph was hated by his brothers and while they were in the fields one day they decided to sell Joseph to some traders who were on their way to Egypt. Eventually, Joseph became second in command to the Pharaoh and during a time of famine, his brothers came to Egypt looking for food. (For the longer version, read Genesis 37-50.) Eventually, the entire families of these twelve boys reunited and moved into Egypt, and were fruitful and multiplied greatly. Many years later the generation of Joseph and his brothers died off and now the Israelites were stuck in Egypt doing hard labor. This is when God calls Moses to get the Israelites out of Egypt and back to the Promised Land – the land of Israel.

Once the Israelites (or Hebrews) made it out of Egypt they spent 40 years wandering in the desert with Moses (read Exodus for this story.) During this time, God gave them instructions on building a great tent where they could worship God and make sacrifices. **Exodus 25:8-9 says "Let them construct a sanctuary for Me, that I may dwell among them. According to all that I am going to show you, as the pattern of the tabernacle and the pattern of all its furniture, just so you shall construct it."** The Tabernacle (which was what the tent was called) would be moved from place to place as they moved throughout the wilderness and served as a place of worship and sacrifice for more than 350 years.

As history continued, around 1,000 B.C. King David, living in the heart of **Jerusalem**, wanted to build God a permanent place of worship; but because David spent much of his life at war, God refused his request and gave the task to his son Solomon. **2 Samuel 7:1-15: Now it came about when the king lived in his house, and the Lord had given him rest on every side from all his enemies, that the king said to Nathan the prophet, "See now, I dwell in a house of cedar, but the ark of God dwells within tent curtains." Nathan said to the king, "Go, do all that is in your mind, for the Lord is with you." But in the same night the word of the Lord came to Nathan, saying, "Go and say to My servant David, 'Thus says the Lord, "Are you the one who should build Me a house to dwell in? For I have not dwelt in a house since the day I brought up the sons of Israel from Egypt, even to this day; but I have been moving about in a tent, even in a tabernacle. Wherever I have gone with all the sons of Israel, did I speak a word with one of the tribes of Israel, which I commanded to shepherd My people Israel, saying, 'Why have you not built Me a house of cedar?' Now therefore, thus you shall say to My servant David, 'Thus says the Lord of hosts, I took you from the pasture, from following the sheep, to be ruler over My people Israel. I have been with you wherever you have gone and have cut off all your enemies from before you; and I will make you a great name, like the names of the great men who are on the earth. I will also appoint a place for My people Israel and will plant them, that they may live in their own place and not be disturbed again, nor will the wicked afflict them any more as formerly, even from the day that I commanded judges to be over My people Israel; and I will give you rest from all your enemies. The Lord also declares to you that the Lord will make a house for you. When your days are complete and you lie down with your fathers, I will raise up your descendant after you, who will come forth from you, and I will establish his kingdom. He shall build a house for My name, and I will establish the throne of his kingdom forever. I will be a father to him and he will be a son to Me; when he commits iniquity, I will correct him with the rod of men and the strokes of the sons of men, but My lovingkindness shall not depart from him, as I took it away from Saul, whom I removed from before you."**

David's son Solomon was chosen to build the first temple which was completed in approximately 950 B.C. (For details of this story read 1 Kings). **1 Kings 6:11-13 says: Now the word of the Lord came to Solomon saying, "Concerning this house which you are building, if you will walk in My statutes and execute My ordinances and keep all My commandments by walking in them, then I will carry out My word with you which**

I spoke to David your father. I will dwell among the sons of Israel, and will not forsake My people Israel."

This **Temple** stood for four hundred years until Israel turned their back on God and Solomon's temple was destroyed in 586 B.C. by the Babylonians. **2 Kings 24:10-14 says: At that time the servants of Nebuchadnezzar king of Babylon went up to Jerusalem, and the city came under siege. And Nebuchadnezzar the king of Babylon came to the city, while his servants were besieging it. Jehoiachin the king of Judah went out to the king of Babylon, he and his mother and his servants and his captains and his officials. So the king of Babylon took him captive in the eighth year of his reign. He carried out from there all the treasures of the house of the Lord, and the treasures of the king's house, and cut in pieces all the vessels of gold which Solomon king of Israel had made in the temple of the Lord, just as the Lord had said. Then he led away into exile all Jerusalem and all the captains and all the mighty men of valor, ten thousand captives, and all the craftsmen and the smiths. None remained except the poorest people of the land.**

Fifty years later, many of the Israelites returned to **Jerusalem** and began to rebuild the temple under Ezra and Nehemiah. **Ezra 3:11-13** says**: And they sang one to another in praising and giving thanks unto Jehovah, saying, For he is good, for his lovingkindness endureth for ever toward Israel. And all the people shouted with a great shout, when they praised Jehovah, because the foundation of the house of Jehovah was laid. But many of the priests and Levites and heads of fathers' houses, the old men that had seen the first house, when the foundation of this house was laid before their eyes, wept with a loud voice; and many shouted aloud for joy, so that the people could not discern the noise of the shout of joy from the noise of the weeping of the people, for the people shouted with a loud shout, and the noise was heard afar off.** This rebuilt temple stood for the next few hundred years until 19 B.C when Herod decided to build an inconceivable temple for the Jewish people. Unfortunately it was built for the wrong reasons and in A.D. 70, six years after it was completed, it was totally destroyed by the Romans. That was the last Jewish temple ever built on that site.

In 638, the Muslims took over the temple mount site and built the Dome of the Rock and the al-Aqsa mosque. In 1948 Israel was established as an independent state and yet, as of today, the **Temple** Mount is still controlled by the Muslims. Once we begin to realize how important this land is to the Jewish people and to the Muslim people, we can start to see why there is so much conflict in the Middle East today.

Herod's temple was built at the time of Jesus, therefore as Christians, this historical site is important to us. The Bible is filled with verses that put Jesus, the disciples, and Paul right in the heart of **Jerusalem** on and around the **Temple** Mount. Just outside the city wall is the **Mount of Olives**, the Garden of **Gethsemane**, the Garden **Tomb**, and **Golgotha**. North of **Jerusalem** is where Jesus walked through towns like **Capernaum**, **Caeserea Philippi**, **Nazareth** and **Bethlehem**. We see in Acts the travels of the Apostle Paul in **Caeserea** by the sea. When we can see that these are true, historical places, it builds our faith to a new level.

As you go from place to place and read the verses we have attached to each site you will be amazed at how reading the Bible will come alive to you. We hope you enjoy this book as much as we enjoyed seeing the beautiful, historical, Holy Land.

For a more in depth historical study of the Temple, a great source is "The Splendor of the Temple" written by Alec Garrard.

Todd Bolen/BiblePlaces.com

BETHANY

Interesting Facts:

• *Lazarus, Mary and Martha lived in Bethany.*

• *Lazurus was raised from the dead in Bethany.*

Mark 11:1-10 As they approached Jerusalem, at Bethphage and **Bethany**, near the Mount of Olives, He sent two of His disciples, and said to them, "Go into the village opposite you, and immediately as you enter it, you will find a colt tied there, on which no one yet has ever sat; untie it and bring it here. "If anyone says to you, 'Why are you doing this?' you say, 'The Lord has need of it'; and immediately he will send it back here." They went

Todd Bolen/BiblePlaces.com
Image on page 12 - Todd Bolen/BiblePlaces.com

away and found a colt tied at the door, outside in the street; and they untied it. Some of the bystanders were saying to them, "What are you doing, untying the colt?" They spoke to them just as Jesus had told them, and they gave them permission. They brought the colt to Jesus and put their coats on it; and He sat on it. And many spread their coats in the road, and others spread leafy branches which they had cut from the fields. Those who went in front and those who followed were shouting: "Hosanna! Blessed is He who comes in the name of the Lord; blessed is the coming kingdom of our father David; Hosanna in the highest!"

Mark 11:11-14 Jesus entered Jerusalem and came into the temple; and after looking around at everything, He left for **Bethany** with the twelve, since it was already late. On the next day, when they had left **Bethany**, He became hungry. Seeing at a distance a fig tree in leaf, He went to see if perhaps He would find anything on it; and when He came to it, He found nothing but leaves, for it was not the season for figs. He said to it, "May no one ever eat fruit from you again!" And His disciples were listening.

John 11:1-43 Now a certain man was sick, Lazarus of **Bethany**, the village of Mary and her sister Martha. It was the Mary who anointed the Lord with ointment, and wiped His feet with her hair, whose brother Lazarus was sick. So the sisters sent word to Him, saying, "Lord, behold, he whom You love is sick." But when Jesus heard this, He said, "This sickness is not to end in death, but for the glory of God, so that the Son of God may be glorified by it." Now Jesus loved Martha and her sister and Lazarus. So when He heard that he was sick, He then stayed two days longer in the place where He was. Then after this He said to the disciples, "Let us go to Judea again." The disciples said to Him, "Rabbi, the Jews were just now seeking to stone You, and are You going there again?" Jesus answered, "Are there not twelve hours in the day? If anyone walks in the day, he does not stumble, because he sees the light of this world. But if anyone walks in the night, he stumbles, because the

Todd Bolen/BiblePlaces.com

light is not in him." This He said, and after that He said to them, "Our friend Lazarus has fallen asleep; but I go, so that I may awaken him out of sleep." The disciples then said to Him, "Lord, if he has fallen asleep, he will recover." Now Jesus had spoken of his death, but they thought that He was speaking of literal sleep. So Jesus then said to them plainly, "Lazarus is dead, and I am glad for your sakes that I was not there, so that you may believe; but let us go to him." Therefore Thomas, who is called Didymus, said to his fellow disciples, "Let us also go, so that we may die with Him." So when Jesus came, He found that he had already been in the tomb four days. Now **Bethany** was near Jerusalem, about two miles off; and many of the Jews had come to Martha and Mary, to console them concerning their brother. Martha therefore, when she heard that Jesus was coming, went to meet Him, but Mary stayed at the house. Martha then said to Jesus, "Lord, if You had been here, my brother would not have died. Even now I know that whatever You ask of God, God will give You." Jesus said to her, "Your brother will rise again." Martha said to Him, "I know that he will rise again in the resurrection on the last day." Jesus said to her, "I am the resurrection and the life; he who believes in Me will live even if he dies, and everyone who lives and believes in Me will never die. Do you believe this?" She said to Him, "Yes, Lord; I have believed that You are the Christ, the Son of God, even He who comes into the world." When she had said this, she went away and called Mary her sister, saying secretly, "The Teacher is here and is calling for you." And when she heard it, she got up quickly and was coming to Him. Now Jesus had not yet come into the village, but was still in the place where Martha met Him. Then the Jews who were with her in the house, and consoling her, when they saw that Mary got up quickly and went out, they followed her, supposing that she was going to the tomb to weep there. Therefore, when Mary came where Jesus was, she saw Him, and fell at His feet, saying to Him, "Lord, if You had been here, my brother would not have died." When Jesus therefore saw her weeping, and the Jews who came with her also weeping, He was deeply moved in spirit and was troubled, and said, "Where have you laid him?" They said to Him, "Lord, come and see." Jesus wept. So the Jews were saying, "See how He loved him!" But some of them said, "Could not this man, who opened the eyes of the blind man, have kept this man also from dying?" So Jesus, again being deeply moved within, came to the tomb. Now it was a cave, and a stone was lying against it. Jesus said, "Remove the stone." Martha, the sister of the deceased, said to Him, "Lord, by this time there will be a stench, for he has been dead four days." Jesus said to her, "Did I not say to you that if you believe, you will see the glory of God?" So they removed the stone. Then Jesus raised His eyes, and said, "Father, I thank You that You have heard Me. I knew that You always hear Me; but because of the people standing around I said it, so that they may believe that You sent Me." When He had said these things, He cried out with a loud voice, "Lazarus, come forth."

John 12:1-8 Jesus, therefore, six days before the Passover, came to **Bethany** where Lazarus was, whom Jesus had raised from the dead. So they made Him a supper there, and Martha was serving; but Lazarus was one of those reclining at the table with Him. Mary then took a pound of very costly perfume of pure nard, and anointed the feet of Jesus and wiped His feet with her hair; and the house was filled with the fragrance of the perfume. But Judas Iscariot, one of His disciples, who was intending to betray Him, said, "Why was this perfume not sold for three hundred denarii and given to poor people?" Now he said this, not because he was concerned about the poor, but because he was a thief, and as he had the money box, he used to pilfer what was put into it. Therefore Jesus said, "Let her alone, so that she may keep it for the day of My burial. For you always have the poor with you, but you do not always have Me."

Todd Bolen/BiblePlaces.com

BETHLEHEM

Interesting Facts:

- *Rachel died from childbirth with her son Benjamin and was buried on the way to Bethlehem.*

- *Naomi and her husband lived in Bethlehem before the famine that took them to Moab.*

- *Ruth followed Naomi back to Bethlehem to live where she met Boaz.*

- *David and his family lived in Bethlehem.*

- *3 mighty men drew water from a well in Bethlehem for David as he was in hiding.*

- *Bethlehem was the location of Jesus' birth prophesied in the Old Testament in Micah.*

- *Jesus was born in Bethlehem.*

- *Herod was outraged and killed all the male children under two years old in Bethlehem.*

David Bivin/LifeintheHolyLand.com
Image on page 18 - David Bivin/LifeintheHolyLand.com

Genesis 35:16-21 Then they journeyed from Bethel; and when there was still some distance to go to Ephrath, Rachel began to give birth and she suffered severe labor. When she was in severe labor the midwife said to her, "Do not fear, for now you have another son." It came about as her soul was departing (for she died), that she named him Ben-oni; but his father called him Benjamin. So Rachel died and was buried on the way to Ephrath (that is, **Bethlehem**). Jacob set up a pillar over her grave; that is the pillar of Rachel's grave to this day. Then Israel journeyed on and pitched his tent beyond the tower of Eder.

Todd Bolen/BiblePlaces.com

Ruth 1:1-5 Now it came about in the days when the judges governed, that there was a famine in the land. And a certain man of **Bethlehem** in Judah went to sojourn in the land of Moab with his wife and his two sons. The name of the man was Elimelech, and the name of his wife, Naomi; and the names of his two sons were Mahlon and Chilion, Ephrathites of **Bethlehem** in Judah. Now they entered the land of Moab and remained there. Then Elimelech, Naomi's husband, died; and she was left with her two sons. They took for themselves Moabite women as wives; the name of the one was Orpah and the name of the other Ruth. And they lived there about ten years. Then both Mahlon and Chilion also died, and the woman was bereft of her two children and her husband.

Ruth 1:14-22 And they lifted up their voices and wept again; and Orpah kissed her mother-in-law, but Ruth clung to her. Then she said, "Behold, your sister-in-law has gone

קבר רחל

Todd Bolen/BiblePlaces.com

back to her people and her gods; return after your sister-in-law." But Ruth said, "Do not urge me to leave you or turn back from following you; for where you go, I will go, and where you lodge, I will lodge. Your people shall be my people, and your God, my God. "Where you die, I will die, and there I will be buried. Thus may the Lord do to me, and worse, if anything but death parts you and me." When she saw that she was determined to go with her, she said no more to her. So they both went until they came to **Bethlehem**. And when they had come to **Bethlehem**, all the city was stirred because of them, and the women said, "Is this Naomi?" She said to them, "Do not call me Naomi; call me Mara, for the Almighty has dealt very bitterly with me. I went out full, but the Lord has brought me back empty. Why do you call me Naomi, since the Lord has witnessed against me and the Almighty has afflicted me?" So Naomi returned, and with her Ruth the Moabitess, her daughter-in-law, who returned from the land of Moab. And they came to **Bethlehem** at the beginning of barley harvest.

1 Samuel 16:1-5 Now the Lord said to Samuel, "How long will you grieve over Saul, since I have rejected him from being king over Israel? Fill your horn with oil and go; I will send you to Jesse the **Bethlehemite**, for I have selected a king for Myself among his sons." But Samuel said, "How can I go? When Saul hears of it, he will kill me." And the Lord said, "Take a heifer with you and say, 'I have come to sacrifice to the Lord.' "You

Todd Bolen/BiblePlaces.com

shall invite Jesse to the sacrifice, and I will show you what you shall do; and you shall anoint for Me the one whom I designate to you." So Samuel did what the Lord said, and came to **Bethlehem**. And the elders of the city came trembling to meet him and said, "Do you come in peace?" He said, "In peace; I have come to sacrifice to the Lord. Consecrate yourselves and come with me to the sacrifice." He also consecrated Jesse and his sons and

Todd Bolen/BiblePlaces.com

invited them to the sacrifice.

2 Samuel 23:13-17 Then three of the thirty chief men went down and came to David in the harvest time to the cave of Adullam, while the troop of the Philistines was camping in the valley of Rephaim. David was then in the stronghold, while the garrison of the Philistines was then in **Bethlehem**. David had a craving and said, "Oh that someone would give me water to drink from the well of **Bethlehem** which is by the gate!" So the three mighty men broke through the camp of the Philistines, and drew water from the well of **Bethlehem** which was by the gate, and took it and brought it to David. Nevertheless he would not drink it, but poured it out to the Lord; and he said, "Be it far from me, O Lord, that I should do this. Shall I drink the blood of the men who went in jeopardy of their lives?" Therefore he would not drink it. These things the three mighty men did.

Todd Bolen/BiblePlaces.com

Micah 5:2 "But as for you, **Bethlehem** Ephrathah, too little to be among the clans of Judah, from you One will go forth for Me to be ruler in Israel. His goings forth are from long ago, from the days of eternity." (NOTE: This is prophecy regarding the birth of Jesus in **Bethlehem**.)

Matthew 2:1-8 Now after Jesus was born in **Bethlehem** of Judea in the days of Herod the king, magi from the east arrived in Jerusalem, saying, "Where is He who has been born King of the Jews? For we saw His star in the east and have come to worship Him." When Herod the king heard this, he was troubled, and all Jerusalem with him. Gathering together all the chief priests and scribes of the people, he inquired of them where the Messiah was to be born. They said to him, "In **Bethlehem** of Judea; for this is what has been written by the prophet: 'And you, **Bethlehem**, land of Judah, are by no means least

among the leaders of Judah; for out of you shall come forth a Ruler Who will shepherd My people Israel.' " Then Herod secretly called the magi and determined from them the exact time the star appeared. And he sent them to **Bethlehem** and said, "Go and search carefully for the Child; and when you have found Him, report to me, so that I too may come and worship Him."

Matthew 2:16-18 Then when Herod saw that he had been tricked by the magi, he became very enraged, and sent and slew all the male children who were in **Bethlehem** and all its vicinity, from two years old and under, according to the time which he had determined from the magi. Then what had been spoken through Jeremiah the prophet was fulfilled: "A voice was heard in Ramah, weeping and great mourning, Rachel weeping for her children; and she refused to be comforted, because they were no more."

Luke 2:4-16 Joseph also went up from Galilee, from the city of Nazareth, to Judea, to the city of David which is called **Bethlehem**, because he was of the house and family of David, in order to register along with Mary, who was engaged to him, and was with child. While they were there, the days were completed for her to give birth. And she gave birth to her firstborn son; and she wrapped Him in cloths, and laid Him in a manger, because there was no room for them in the inn. In the same region there were some shepherds staying out in the fields and keeping watch over their flock by night. And an angel of the Lord suddenly stood before them, and the glory of the Lord shone around them; and they were terribly frightened. But the angel said to them, "Do not be afraid; for behold, I bring you good news of great joy which will be for all the people; for today in the city of David there has been born for you a Savior, who is Christ the Lord. "this will be a sign for you: you will find a baby wrapped in cloths and lying in a manger." And suddenly there appeared with the angel a multitude of the heavenly host praising God and saying, "Glory to God in the highest, and on earth peace among men with whom He is pleased." When the angels had gone away from them into heaven, the shepherds began saying to one another, "Let us go straight to **Bethlehem** then, and see this thing that has happened which the Lord has made known to us." So they came in a hurry and found their way to Mary and Joseph, and the baby as He lay in the manger.

25

BETHSAIDA

Interesting Facts:

- *The disciples were on their way to Bethsaida when a storm arose and Jesus walked on the water.*

- *Jesus withdrew by Himself to Bethsaida where the crowds followed Him.*

- *Andrew, Peter and Philip were from Bethsaida.*

Mark 6:45-52 Immediately Jesus made His disciples get into the boat and go ahead of Him to the other side to **Bethsaida**, while He Himself was sending the crowd away. After bidding them farewell, He left for the mountain to pray. When it was evening, the boat was in the middle of the sea, and He was alone on the land. Seeing them straining at the oars, for the wind was against them, at about the fourth watch of the night He came to them, walking on the sea; and He intended to pass by them. But when they saw Him walking on the sea, they supposed that it was a ghost, and cried out; for they all saw Him and were terrified. But immediately He spoke with them and said to them, "Take courage; it is I, do not be afraid." Then He got into the boat with them, and the wind stopped; and they were utterly astonished, for they had not gained any insight from the incident of the loaves, but their heart was hardened.

Luke 9:10-11 When the apostles returned, they gave an account

Todd Bolen/BiblePlaces.com

to Him of all that they had done. Taking them with Him, He withdrew by Himself to a city called **Bethsaida**. But the crowds were aware of this and followed Him; and welcoming them, He began speaking to them about the kingdom of God and curing those who had need of healing.

John 1:43-45 The next day He purposed to go into Galilee, and He found Philip. And Jesus said to him, "Follow Me." Now Philip was from **Bethsaida**, of the city of Andrew and Peter. Philip found Nathanael and said to him, "We have found Him of whom Moses in the Law and also the Prophets wrote—Jesus of Nazareth, the son of Joseph."

Todd Bolen/BiblePlaces.com

Todd Bolen/BiblePlaces.com

BETH SHEAN
(or spelled BETH-SHAN)

Interesting Facts:

• *Saul and his sons were killed and their bodies fastened to the wall at Beth-Shan.*

Judges 1:27 But Manasseh did not take possession of **Beth-shean** and its villages, or Taanach and its villages, or the inhabitants of Dor and its villages, or the inhabitants of Ibleam and its villages, or the inhabitants of Megiddo and its villages; so the Canaanites persisted in living in that land.

1 Samuel 31:8-13 It came about on the next day when the Philistines came to strip the slain, that they found Saul and his three sons fallen on Mount Gilboa. They cut off his head and stripped off his weapons, and sent them throughout the land of the Philistines, to carry the good news to the house of their idols and to the people. They put his weapons in the temple of Ashtaroth, and they fastened his body to the wall of **Beth-shan**. Now when the inhabitants of Jabesh-gilead heard what the Philistines had done to Saul, all the valiant men rose and walked all night, and took the body of Saul and the bodies of his sons from the wall of **Beth-shan**, and they came to Jabesh and burned them there. They took their bones and buried them under the tamarisk tree at Jabesh, and fasted seven days.

Todd Bolen/BiblePlaces.com
Image on page 30 - Todd Bolen/BiblePlaces.com

CAESAREA

Interesting facts:

• *Philip preached until he reached Caesarea.*

• *When the jews tried to kill Paul for preaching, the disciples took him to Caesarea and sent him away from there on a ship to Tarsus.*

• *Cornelius was from Caesarea.*

• *Peter came to Caesarea to meet with Cornielius.*

• *Two hundred soldiers, seventy horsemen and two hundred spearmen escorted Paul to Caesarea when his life was threatened.*

• *Felix left Paul in prison for over two years in Caeserea before he was sent to Rome.*

Acts 8:34-40 The eunuch answered Philip and said, "Please tell me, of whom does the prophet say this? Of himself or of someone else?" Then Philip opened his mouth, and beginning from this Scripture he preached Jesus to him. As they went along the road they came to some water; and the eunuch said, "Look! Water! What prevents

Todd Bolen/BiblePlaces.com
Image on page 32 - Todd Bolen/BiblePlaces.com

Todd Bolen/BiblePlaces.com

me from being baptized?" [And Philip said, "If you believe with all your heart, you may." And he answered and said, "I believe that Jesus Christ is the Son of God."] And he ordered the chariot to stop; and they both went down into the water, Philip as well as the eunuch, and he baptized him. When they came up out of the water, the Spirit of the Lord snatched Philip away; and the eunuch no longer saw him, but went on his way rejoicing. But Philip found himself at Azotus, and as he passed through he kept preaching the gospel to all the cities until he came to **Caesarea**.

Todd Bolen/BiblePlaces.com

Acts 9:26-30 When he (*Paul*) came to Jerusalem, he was trying to associate with the disciples; but they were all afraid of him, not believing that he was a disciple. But Barnabas took hold of him and brought him to the apostles and described to them how he had seen the Lord on the road, and that He had talked to him, and how at Damascus he had spoken out boldly in the name of Jesus. And he was with them, moving about freely in Jerusalem, speaking out boldly in the name of the Lord. And he was talking and arguing with the Hellenistic Jews; but they were attempting to put him to death. But when the brethren learned of it, they brought him down to **Caesarea** and sent him away to Tarsus. (italics ours)

Acts 10:1-6 Now there was a man at **Caesarea** named Cornelius, a centurion of what was called the Italian cohort, a devout man and one who feared God with all his household, and gave many alms to the Jewish people and prayed to God continually. About the ninth hour of the day he clearly saw in a vision an angel of God who had just come in and said to him, "Cornelius!" And fixing his gaze on him and being much alarmed, he said, "What is it, Lord?" And he said

Todd Bolen/BiblePlaces.com

to him, "Your prayers and alms have ascended as a memorial before God. Now dispatch some men to Joppa and send for a man named Simon, who is also called Peter; he is staying with a tanner named Simon, whose house is by the sea."

Acts 10:24-33 On the following day he entered **Caesarea**. Now Cornelius was waiting for them and had called together his relatives and close friends. When Peter entered, Cornelius met him, and fell at his feet and worshiped him. But Peter raised him up, saying, "Stand up; I too am just a man." As he talked with him, he entered and found many people assembled. And he said to them, "You yourselves know

Todd Bolen/BiblePlaces.com

how unlawful it is for a man who is a Jew to associate with a foreigner or to visit him; and yet God has shown me that I should not call any man unholy or unclean. That is why I came without even raising any objection when I was sent for. So I ask for what reason you have sent for me." Cornelius

Todd Bolen/BiblePlaces.com

said, "Four days ago to this hour, I was praying in my house during the ninth hour; and behold, a man stood before me in shining garments, and he said, 'Cornelius, your prayer has been heard and your alms have been remembered before God. Therefore send to Joppa and invite Simon, who is also called Peter, to come to you; he is staying at the house of Simon the tanner by the sea.' So I sent for you immediately, and you have been kind enough to come. Now then, we are all here present before God to hear all that you have been commanded by the Lord."

Todd Bolen/BiblePlaces.com

Acts 11:9-12 "But a voice from heaven answered a second time, 'What God has cleansed, no longer consider unholy.' "This happened three times, and everything was drawn back up into the sky. "And behold, at that moment three men appeared at the house in which we were staying, having been sent to me from **Caesarea**. "The Spirit told me to go with them without misgivings. These six brethren also went with me and we entered the man's house.

Acts 12:18-19 Now when day came, there was no small disturbance among the soldiers as to what could have become of Peter. When Herod had searched for him and had not found him, he examined the guards and ordered that they be led away to execution. Then he went down from Judea to **Caesarea** and was spending time there.

Acts 18:19-23 They came to Ephesus, and he left them there. Now he (*Paul*) himself entered the synagogue and reasoned with the Jews. When they asked him to stay for a longer time, he did not consent, but taking leave of them and saying, "I will return to you again if God wills," he set sail from Ephesus. When he had landed at **Caesarea**, he went up and greeted the church, and went down to Antioch. And having spent some time there, he left and passed successively through the Galatian region and Phrygia, strengthening all the disciples. (italics ours)

Todd Bolen/BiblePlaces.com

Acts 21:7-8 When we had finished the voyage from Tyre, we arrived at Ptolemais, and after greeting the brethren, we stayed with them for a day. On the next day we left and came to **Caesarea**, and entering the house of Philip the evangelist, who was one of the seven, we stayed with him.

Todd Bolen/BiblePlaces.com

Acts 23:16-24 But the son of Paul's sister heard of their ambush, and he came and entered the barracks and told Paul. Paul called one of the centurions to him and said, "Lead this young man to the commander, for he has something to report to him." So he took him and led him to the commander and said, "Paul the prisoner called me to him and asked me to

lead this young man to you since he has something to tell you." The commander took him by the hand and stepping aside, began to inquire of him privately, "What is it that you have to report to me?" And he said, "The Jews have agreed to ask you to bring Paul down tomorrow to the Council, as though they were going to inquire somewhat more thoroughly about him. So do not listen to them, for more than forty of them are lying in wait for him who have bound themselves under a curse not to eat or drink until they slay him; and now they are ready and waiting for the promise from you." So the commander let the young man go, instructing him, "Tell no one that you have notified me of these things." And he called to him two of the centurions and said, "Get two hundred soldiers ready by the third hour of the night to proceed to **Caesarea**, with seventy horsemen and two hundred spearmen." They were also to provide mounts to put Paul on and bring him safely to Felix the governor.

Acts 23:31-35 So the soldiers, in accordance with their orders, took Paul and brought him by night to Antipatris. But the next day, leaving the horsemen to go on with him, they returned to the barracks. When these had come to **Caesarea** and delivered the letter to the governor, they also presented Paul to him. When he had read it, he asked from what province he was, and when he learned that he was from Cilicia, he said, "I will give you a hearing after your accusers arrive also," giving orders for him to be kept in Herod's Praetorium.

Acts 25:1-13 Festus then, having arrived in the province, three days later went up to Jerusalem from **Caesarea**. And the chief priests and the leading men of the Jews brought charges against Paul, and they were urging him, requesting a concession against Paul, that he might have him brought to

Jerusalem (at the same time, setting an ambush to kill him on the way). Festus then answered that Paul was being kept in custody at **Caesarea** and that he himself was about to leave shortly. "Therefore," he said, "let the influential men among you go there with me, and if there is anything wrong about the man, let them prosecute him." After he had spent not more than eight or ten days among them, he went down to

Todd Bolen/BiblePlaces.com

Caesarea, and on the next day he took his seat on the tribunal and ordered Paul to be brought. After Paul arrived, the Jews who had come down from Jerusalem stood around him, bringing many and serious charges against him which they could not prove, while Paul said in his own defense, "I have committed no offense either against the Law of the Jews or against the temple or against Caesar." But Festus, wishing to do the Jews a favor, answered Paul and said, "Are you willing to go up to Jerusalem and stand trial before me on these charges?" But Paul said, "I am standing before Caesar's tribunal, where I ought to be tried. I have done no wrong to the Jews, as you also very well know. If, then, I am a wrongdoer and have committed anything worthy of death, I do not refuse to die; but if none of those things is true of which these men accuse me, no one can hand me over to them. I appeal to Caesar." Then when Festus had conferred with his council, he answered, "You have appealed to Caesar, to Caesar you shall go." Now when several days had elapsed, King Agrippa and Bernice arrived at **Caesarea** and paid their respects to Festus.

CAESAREA PHILIPPI

Interesting Fact:

- *Jesus asked the disciples "Who do people say that the Son of Man is?" near Caesarea Philippi.*

Matthew 16:13-18 Now when Jesus came into the district of **Caesarea Philippi**, He was asking His disciples, "Who do people say that the Son of Man is?" And they said, "Some say John the Baptist; and others, Elijah; but still others, Jeremiah, or one of the prophets." He said to them, "But who do you say that I am?" Simon Peter answered, "You are the Christ, the Son of the living God." And Jesus said to him, "Blessed are you, Simon Barjona, because flesh and blood did not reveal this to you, but My Father who is in heaven. "I also say to you that you are Peter, and upon this rock I will build My church; and the gates of Hades will not overpower it.

Mark 8:27-30 Jesus went out, along with His disciples, to the villages of **Caesarea Philippi**; and on the way He questioned His disciples, saying to them, "Who do people say that I am?" They told Him, saying, "John the Baptist; and others say Elijah; but others, one of the prophets." And He continued by questioning them, "But who do you say that I am?" Peter answered and said to Him, "You are the Christ." And He warned them to tell no one about Him.

Todd Bolen/BiblePlaces.com
Image on page 40 - Todd Bolen/BiblePlaces.com

CAIAPHAS' HOUSE

Interesting Facts:

- *The priests and elders were gathered in Caiaphas' court to plot how to seize and kill Jesus.*

- *Jesus was led to Caiaphas' House after He was arrested.*

- *Peter followed Jesus to the courtyard of Caiaphas where he denied three times that he knew Jesus.*

Matthew 26:1-5 When Jesus had finished all these words, He said to His disciples, "You know that after two days the Passover is coming, and the Son of Man is to be handed over for crucifixion." Then the chief priests and the elders of the people were gathered together in the court of the high priest, named **Caiaphas**; and they plotted together to seize Jesus by stealth and kill Him. But they were saying, "Not during the festival, otherwise a riot might occur among the people."

Matthew 26:57-58 Those who had seized Jesus led Him away to **Caiaphas**, the high priest, where the scribes and the elders were gathered together. But Peter was following Him at a distance as far

Todd Bolen/BiblePlaces.com
Image on page 42 - Todd Bolen/BiblePlaces.com

as the courtyard of the high priest, and entered in, and sat down with the officers to see the outcome.

John 11:47-53 Therefore the chief priests and the Pharisees convened a council, and were saying, "What are we doing? For this man is performing many signs. If we let Him go on like this, all men will believe in Him, and the Romans will come and take away both our place and our nation." But one of them, **Caiaphas**, who was high priest that year, said to them, "You know nothing at all, nor do you take into account that it is expedient for you that one man die for the people, and that the whole nation not perish." Now he did not say this on his own initiative, but being high priest that year, he prophesied that Jesus was going to die for the nation, and not for the nation only, but in order that He might also gather together into one the children of God who are scattered abroad. So from that day on they planned together to kill Him.

John 18:12-14 So the Roman cohort and the commander and the officers of the Jews, arrested Jesus and bound Him, and led Him to Annas first; for he was father-in-law of **Caiaphas**, who was high priest that year. Now **Caiaphas** was the one who had advised the Jews that it was expedient for one man to die on behalf of the people. John 18:15-18 Simon Peter was following Jesus, and so was another disciple. Now that disciple was known to the high priest, and entered with Jesus into the

court of the high priest, but Peter was standing at the door outside. So the other disciple, who was known to the high priest, went out and spoke to the doorkeeper, and brought Peter in. Then the slave-girl who kept the door said to Peter, "You are not also one of this man's disciples, are you?" He said, "I am not." Now the slaves and the officers were standing there, having made a charcoal fire, for it was cold and they were warming themselves; and Peter was also with them, standing and warming himself. John 18:25-27 Now Simon Peter was standing and warming himself. So they said to him, "You are not also one of His disciples, are you?" He denied it, and said, "I am not." One of the slaves of the high priest, being a relative of the one whose ear Peter cut off, said, "Did I not see you in the garden with Him?" Peter then denied it again, and immediately a rooster crowed.

John 18:19-24 The high priest then questioned Jesus about His disciples, and about His teaching. Jesus answered him, "I have spoken openly to the world; I always taught in synagogues and in the temple, where all the Jews come together; and I spoke nothing in secret. Why do you question Me? Question those who have heard what I spoke to them; they know what I said." When He had said this, one of the officers standing nearby struck

Todd Bolen/BiblePlaces.com

Jesus, saying, "Is that the way You answer the high priest?" Jesus answered him, "If I have spoken wrongly, testify of the wrong; but if rightly, why do you strike Me?" So Annas sent Him bound to **Caiaphas** the high priest.

John 18:28-38 Then they led Jesus from **Caiaphas** into the Praetorium, and it was early; and they themselves did not enter into the Praetorium so that they would not be defiled, but might eat the Passover. Therefore Pilate went out to them and said, "What accusation do you bring against this Man?" They answered and said to him, "If this Man were not an evildoer,

Todd Bolen/BiblePlaces.com

we would not have delivered Him to you." So Pilate said to them, "Take Him yourselves, and judge Him according to your law." The Jews said to him, "We are not permitted to put anyone to death," to fulfill the word of Jesus which He spoke, signifying by what kind of death He was about to die. Therefore Pilate entered again into the Praetorium, and summoned Jesus and said to Him, "Are You the King of the Jews?" Jesus answered, "Are you saying this on your own initiative, or did others tell you about Me?" Pilate answered, "I am not a Jew, am I? Your own nation and the chief priests delivered You to me; what have You done?" Jesus answered, "My kingdom is not of this world. If My kingdom were of this world, then My servants would be fighting so that I would not be handed over to the Jews; but as it is, My kingdom is not of this realm." Therefore Pilate said to Him, "So You are a king?" Jesus answered, "You say correctly that I am a king. For this I have been born, and for this I have come into the world, to testify to the truth. Everyone who is of the truth hears My voice." Pilate said to Him, "What is truth?" And when he had said this, he went out again to the Jews and said to them, "I find no guilt in Him."

Todd Bolen/BiblePlaces.com

CAPERNAUM

Interesting Facts:

- *After Jesus heard John was taken into custody, He settled in Capernaum.*

- *A Centurion's servant was healed after speaking with Jesus in Capernaum.*

- *Peter's home was in Capernaum.*

- *Jesus healed Peter's mother in law at his house in Capernaum.*

- *Jesus taught in the synagogue in Capernaum and cast out a demon there.*

- *The paralytic was lowered down from the roof where Jesus was teaching and he was healed in Capernaum.*

- *Jesus walked on the water as the disciples were in the boat on their way to Capernaum.*

Matthew 4:12-13 Now when Jesus heard that John had been taken into custody, He withdrew into Galilee; and leaving Nazareth, He came and settled in **Capernaum**, which is by the

Todd Bolen/BiblePlaces.com
Image on page 48 - Todd Bolen/BiblePlaces.com

sea, in the region of Zebulun and Naphtali.

Todd Bolen/BiblePlaces.com

Matthew 8:5-13 And when Jesus entered **Capernaum**, a centurion came to Him, imploring Him, and saying, "Lord, my servant is lying paralyzed at home, fearfully tormented." Jesus said to him, "I will come and heal him." But the centurion said, "Lord, I am not worthy for You to come under my roof, but just say the word, and my servant will be healed. For I also am a man under authority, with soldiers under me; and I say to this one, 'Go!' and he goes, and to another, 'Come!' and he comes, and to my slave, 'Do this!' and he does it." Now when Jesus heard this, He marveled and said to those who were following, "Truly I say to you, I have not found such great faith with anyone in Israel. I say to you that many will come from east and west, and recline at the table with Abraham, Isaac and Jacob in the kingdom of heaven; but the sons of the kingdom will be cast out into the outer darkness; in that place there will be weeping and gnashing of teeth." And Jesus said to the centurion, "Go; it shall be done for you as you have believed." And the servant was healed that very moment.

Matthew 8:14-17 When Jesus came into Peter's home, He saw his mother-in-law lying sick in bed with a fever. He touched her hand, and the fever left her; and she got up and waited on Him. When evening came, they brought to Him

Todd Bolen/BiblePlaces.com

many who were demon-possessed; and He cast out the spirits with a word, and healed all who were ill. This was to fulfill what was spoken through Isaiah the prophet: "He Himself took our infirmities and carried away our diseases." (This was in **Capernaum**)

Todd Bolen/BiblePlaces.com

Matthew 11:20-24 Then He began to denounce the cities in which most of His miracles were done, because they did not repent. "Woe to you, Chorazin! Woe to you, Bethsaida! For if the miracles had occurred in Tyre and Sidon which occurred in you, they would have repented long ago in sackcloth and ashes. Nevertheless I say to you, it will be more tolerable for Tyre and Sidon in the day of judgment than for you. And you, **Capernaum**, will not be exalted to heaven, will you? You will descend to Hades; for if the miracles had occurred in Sodom which occurred in you, it would have remained to this day. Nevertheless I say to you that it will be more tolerable for the land of Sodom in the day of judgment, than for you."

Matthew 17:24-27 When they came to **Capernaum**, those who collected the two-drachma tax came to Peter and said, "Does your teacher not pay the two-drachma tax?" He said, "Yes." And when he came into the house, Jesus spoke to him first,

David Bivin/LifeintheHolyLand.com

saying, "What do you think, Simon? From whom do the kings of the earth collect customs or poll-tax, from their sons or from strangers?" When Peter said, "From strangers," Jesus said to him, "Then the sons are exempt. However, so that we do not offend them, go to the sea and throw in a hook, and take the first fish that comes up; and when you open its mouth, you will find a shekel. Take that and give it to them for you and Me."

Mark 1:21-28 They went into **Capernaum**; and immediately on the Sabbath He entered the synagogue and began to teach. They were amazed at His teaching; for He was teaching them as one having authority, and not as the scribes. Just then there was a man in their synagogue with an unclean spirit; and he cried out, saying, "What business do we have with each other, Jesus of Nazareth? Have You come to destroy us? I know who You are—the Holy One of God!" And Jesus rebuked him, saying, "Be quiet, and come out of him!" Throwing him into convulsions, the unclean spirit cried out with a loud voice and came out of him. They were all amazed, so that they debated among themselves, saying, "What is this? A new teaching with authority! He commands even the unclean spirits, and they obey Him." Immediately the news about Him spread everywhere into all the surrounding district of Galilee.

Mark 2:1-12 When He had come back to **Capernaum** several days afterward, it was heard that He was at home. And many were gathered together, so that there was no longer room, not even near the door; and He was speaking the word to them. And they came, bringing to Him a paralytic, carried by four men. Being unable to get to Him because of the crowd, they removed the roof above Him; and when they had dug an opening, they let down the pallet on which the paralytic was lying. And

Jesus seeing their faith said to the paralytic, "Son, your sins are forgiven." But some of the scribes were sitting there and reasoning in their hearts, "Why does this man speak that way? He is blaspheming; who can forgive sins but God alone?" Immediately Jesus, aware in His spirit that they were reasoning that way within themselves, said to them, "Why are you reasoning about these things in your hearts? Which is easier, to say to the paralytic, 'Your sins are forgiven'; or to say, 'Get up, and pick up your pallet and walk'? But so that you may know that the Son of Man has authority on earth to forgive sins"—He said to the paralytic, "I say to you, get up, pick up your pallet and go home." And he got up and immediately picked up the pallet and went out in the sight of everyone, so that they were all amazed and were glorifying God, saying, "We have never seen anything like this."

Mark 9:33-37 They came to **Capernaum**; and when He was in the house, He began to question them, "What were you discussing on the way?" But they kept silent, for on the way they had discussed with one another which of them was the greatest. Sitting down, He called the twelve and said to them, "If anyone wants to be first, he shall be last of all and servant of all." Taking a child, He set him before them, and taking him in His arms, He said to them, "Whoever receives one child like this in My name receives Me;

Todd Bolen/BiblePlaces.com

and whoever receives Me does not receive Me, but Him who sent Me."

Luke 4:31-37 And He came down to **Capernaum**, a city of Galilee, and He was teaching them on the Sabbath; and they were amazed at His teaching, for His message was with authority. In the synagogue there was a man possessed by the spirit of an unclean demon, and he cried out with a loud voice, "Let us alone! What business do we have with each other, Jesus of Nazareth? Have You come to destroy us? I know who You are—the Holy

One of God!" But Jesus rebuked him, saying, "Be quiet and come out of him!" And when the demon had thrown him down in the midst of the people, he came out of him without doing him any harm. And amazement came upon them all, and they began talking with one another saying, "What is this message? For with authority and power He commands the unclean spirits and they come out." And the report about Him was spreading into every locality in the surrounding district.

Luke 7:1-11 When He had completed all His discourse in the hearing of the people, He went to **Capernaum**. And a centurion's slave, who was highly regarded by him, was sick and about to die. When he heard about Jesus, he sent some Jewish elders asking Him to come and save the life of his slave. When they came to Jesus, they earnestly implored Him, saying, "He is worthy for You to grant this to him; for he loves our nation and it was he who built us our synagogue." Now Jesus started on His way with them; and when He was not far from the house, the centurion sent friends, saying to Him, "Lord, do not trouble Yourself further, for I am not worthy for You to come under my roof; for this reason I did not even consider myself worthy to come to You, but just say the word, and my servant will be healed. For I also am a man placed under authority, with soldiers under me; and I say to this one, 'Go!' and he goes, and to another, 'Come!' and he comes, and to my slave, 'Do this!' and he does it." Now when Jesus heard this, He marveled at him, and turned and said to the crowd that was following Him, "I say to you, not even in Israel have I found such great faith." When those who had been sent returned to the house, they found the slave in good health. Soon afterwards He went to a city called Nain; and His disciples were going along with Him, accompanied by a large crowd.

John 2:12 After this He went down to **Capernaum**, He and His mother and His brothers and His disciples; and they stayed there a few days.

John 6:15-21 So Jesus, perceiving that they were intending to come and take Him by force to make Him king, withdrew again to the mountain by Himself alone. Now when evening came, His disciples went down to the sea, and after getting into a boat, they started to cross the sea to **Capernaum**. It had already become dark, and Jesus had not yet come to them. The sea began to be stirred up because a strong wind was blowing. Then, when they had rowed about three or four miles, they saw Jesus walking on the sea and drawing near to the boat; and they were frightened. But He said to them, "It is I; do not be afraid." So they were willing to receive Him into the boat, and immediately the boat was at the land to which they were going.

Todd Bolen/BiblePlaces.com

John 6:58-59 "This is the bread which came down out of heaven; not as the fathers ate and died; he who eats this bread will live forever." These things He said in the synagogue as He taught in **Capernaum**.

Todd Bolen/BiblePlaces.com

THE DEAD SEA (or Salt Sea)

Interesting Facts:

- *Sodom and Gomorrah are near the Dead Sea.*

- *When Lot and Abraham split up, Lot went to the town of Sodom which was by the Dead Sea while Abraham took the land on higher ground.*

Genesis 14:1-3 And it came about in the days of Amraphel king of Shinar, Arioch king of Ellasar, Chedorlaomer king of Elam, and Tidal king of Goiim, that they made war with Bera king of Sodom, and with Birsha king of Gomorrah, Shinab king of Admah, and Shemeber king of Zeboiim, and the king of Bela (that is, Zoar). All these came as allies to the valley of Siddim (that is, the **Salt Sea**).

Joshua 15:2 Their south border was from the lower end of the **Salt Sea**, from the bay that turns to the south.

Genesis 19:26 But his wife, from behind him, looked back, and she became a pillar of salt. (NOTE: Sodom and Gomorrah are close to the **Dead Sea**.)

David Bivin/LifeintheHolyLand.com
Image on page 56 - Todd Bolen/BiblePlaces.com

ENGEDI (or Ein Gedi)

Interesting Facts:

- *David stayed in a cave in Engedi while hiding from Saul.*

- *When Jehoshaphat heard a great multitude was coming against him, he was told they were in Engedi.*

1 Samuel 23:29 David went up from there and stayed in the strongholds of **Engedi**.

Samuel 24:1-4 Now when Saul returned from pursuing the Philistines, he was told, saying, "Behold, David is in the wilderness of **Engedi**." Then Saul took three thousand chosen men from all Israel and went to seek David and his men in front of the Rocks of the Wild Goats. He came to the sheepfolds on the way, where there was a cave; and Saul went in to relieve himself. Now David and his men were sitting in

Todd Bolen/BiblePlaces.com
Image on page 58 - Todd Bolen/BiblePlaces.com

Todd Bolen/BiblePlaces.com

the inner recesses of the cave. The men of David said to him, "Behold, this is the day of which the Lord said to you, 'Behold; I am about to give your enemy into your hand, and you shall do to him as it seems good to you.' " Then David arose and cut off the edge of Saul's robe secretly.

2 Chronicles 20:1-4 Now it came about after this that the sons of Moab and the sons of Ammon, together with some of the Meunites, came to make war against Jehoshaphat. Then some came and reported to Jehoshaphat, saying, "A great multitude is coming against you from beyond the sea, out of Aram and behold, they are in Hazazon-tamar (that is **Engedi**)." Jehoshaphat was afraid and turned his attention to seek the Lord, and proclaimed a fast throughout all Judah. So Judah gathered together to seek help from the Lord; they even came from all the cities of Judah to seek the Lord.

Todd Bolen/BiblePlaces.com

Todd Bolen/BiblePlaces.com

GETHSEMANE

Interesting Facts:

• *This is where Jesus prayed before He was arrested and crucified.*

• *The disciples fell asleep after Jesus asked them to stay awake and pray.*

Matthew 26:36-56 Then Jesus came with them to a place called **Gethsemane**, and said to His disciples, "Sit here while I go over there and pray." And He took with Him Peter and the two sons of Zebedee, and began to be grieved and distressed. Then He said to them, "My soul is deeply grieved, to the point of death; remain here and keep watch with Me." And He went a little beyond them, and fell on His face and prayed, saying, "My Father, if it is possible, let this cup pass from Me; yet not as I will, but as You will." And He came to the disciples and found them sleeping, and said to Peter, "So, you men could not keep watch with Me for one hour? Keep watching and praying that you may not enter into temptation; the spirit is willing, but the flesh is weak." He went away again a second time and prayed, saying, "My Father, if this cannot pass away unless I drink it, Your will be done." Again He came and found them sleeping, for their eyes were heavy. And He left them again, and went away and prayed a third time, saying the same thing once more. Then He came to the disciples and said to them, "Are you still sleeping and resting? Behold, the hour is at hand

Todd Bolen/BiblePlaces.com
Image on page 62 - Todd Bolen/BiblePlaces.com

and the Son of Man is being betrayed into the hands of sinners. "Get up, let us be going; behold, the one who betrays Me is at hand!" While He was still speaking, behold, Judas, one of the twelve, came up accompanied by a large crowd with swords and clubs, who came from the chief priests and elders of the people. Now he who was betraying Him gave them a sign, saying, "Whomever I kiss, He is the one; seize Him." Immediately Judas went to Jesus and said, "Hail, Rabbi!" and kissed Him. And Jesus said to him, "Friend, do what you have come for." Then they came and laid hands on Jesus and seized Him. And behold, one of those who were with Jesus reached and drew out his sword, and struck the slave of the high priest and cut off his ear. Then Jesus said to him, "Put your sword back into its place; for all those who take up the sword shall perish by the sword. Or do you think that I cannot appeal to My Father, and He will at once put at My disposal more than twelve legions of angels? How then will the Scriptures be fulfilled, which say that it must happen this way?" At that time Jesus said to the crowds, "Have you come out with swords and clubs to arrest Me as you would against a robber? Every day I used to sit in the temple teaching and you did not seize Me. But all this has taken place to fulfill the Scriptures of the prophets." Then all the disciples left Him and fled.

Mark 14:32-36 They came to a place named **Gethsemane**; and He said to His disciples, "Sit here until I have prayed." And He took with Him Peter

and James and John, and began to be very distressed and troubled. And He said to them, "My soul is deeply grieved to the point of death; remain here and keep watch." And He went a little beyond them, and fell to the ground and began to pray that if it were possible, the hour might pass Him by. And He was saying, "Abba! Father! All things are possible for You; remove this cup from Me; yet not what I will, but what You will."

Todd Bolen/BiblePlaces.com

Todd Bolen/BiblePlaces.com

GOLGOTHA

Interesting Facts:

• *Jesus was crucified at a place called Golgotha.*

• *Golgotha means "Place of a Skull".*

• *Golgotha was very close to the Garden Tomb.*

Matthew 27:27-37 Then the soldiers of the governor took Jesus into the Praetorium and gathered the whole Roman cohort around Him. They stripped Him and put a scarlet robe on Him. And after twisting together a crown of thorns, they put it on His head, and a reed in His right hand; and they knelt down before Him and mocked Him, saying, "Hail, King of the Jews!" They spat on Him, and took the reed and began to beat Him on the head. After they had mocked Him, they took the scarlet robe off Him and put His own garments back on Him, and led Him away to crucify Him. As they were coming out, they found a man of Cyrene named Simon, whom they pressed into service to bear His cross. And when they came to a place called **Golgotha**, which means Place of a Skull, they gave Him wine to drink mixed with gall; and after tasting it, He was unwilling to drink. And when they had crucified Him, they divided up His garments among themselves by casting lots. And sitting down, they began to keep watch over Him there. And above His head they put up the charge against Him which

David Bivin/LifeintheHolyLand.com
Image on page 66 - Todd Bolen/BiblePlaces.com

read, "THIS IS JESUS THE KING OF THE JEWS."

John 19:17-19 They took Jesus, therefore, and He went out, bearing His own cross, to the place called the Place of a Skull, which is called in Hebrew, **Golgotha**. There they crucified Him, and with Him two other men, one on either side, and Jesus in between. Pilate also wrote an inscription and put it on the cross. It was written, "JESUS THE NAZARENE, THE KING OF THE JEWS."

LC-matpc-03428/www.LifeintheHolyLand.com

Todd Bolen/BiblePlaces.com

Todd Bolen/BiblePlaces.com

HEZEKIAH'S TUNNEL

Interesting Fact:

- *Hezekiah built a tunnel to bring water from one side of the city of Jerusalem to the other.*

- *Hezekiah needed a reliable water supply for Jerusalem.*

- *Hezekiah wanted to prevent the Assyrians from using the Gihon spring so he built a tunnel to redirect the waters to the city.*

2 Kings 20:20-21 Now the rest of the acts of **Hezekiah** and all his might, and how he made the pool and the conduit and brought water into the city, are they not written in the Book of the Chronicles of the Kings of Judah? So **Hezekiah** slept with his fathers, and Manasseh his son became king in his place.

2 Chronicles 32:30 It was **Hezekiah** who stopped the upper outlet of the waters of Gihon and directed them to the west side of the city of David. And **Hezekiah** prospered in all that he did.

Todd Bolen/BiblePlaces.com
Image on page 70 - Todd Bolen/BiblePlaces.com

JERICHO

Interesting Facts:

- *Moses took a census of all the men twenty years and older who would be able to go to war.*

- *Moses went up on Mount Nebo which is opposite of Jericho in order to see the land which God promised to the Israelites before he died.*

- *Joshua took over for Moses and Jericho was a city that was to be destroyed.*

- *Rahab was from Jericho.*

- *Jericho was destroyed when the Israelites walked around the city seven days and when they blew horns on the seventh day - the walls of Jericho fell and the city lay in ruins.*

- *Everyone was destroyed in Jericho except Rahab and her family.*

- *Jesus was in Jericho and healed two blind men who were calling out to Him.*

- *In the story of the good Samaritan – Jesus used Jericho as the place where the man was going to when he was beaten and robbed.*

- *Jesus met Zaccheus in Jericho.*

Image on page 72 - Todd Bolen/BiblePlaces.com

Numbers 22:1 Then the sons of Israel journeyed, and camped in the plains of Moab beyond the Jordan opposite **Jericho**.

Todd Bolen/BiblePlaces.com

Numbers 26:1-4 Then it came about after the plague, that the Lord spoke to Moses and to Eleazar the son of Aaron the priest, saying, "Take a census of all the congregation of the sons of Israel from twenty years old and upward, by their fathers' households, whoever is able to go out to war in Israel." So Moses and Eleazar the priest spoke with them in the plains of Moab by the Jordan at **Jericho**, saying, "Take a census of the people from twenty years old and upward, as the Lord has commanded Moses."

Todd Bolen/BiblePlaces.com

Deuteronomy 32:48-52 The Lord spoke to Moses that very same day, saying, "Go up to this mountain of the Abarim, Mount Nebo, which is in the land of Moab opposite **Jericho**, and look at the land of Canaan, which I am giving to the sons of Israel for a possession. Then die on the mountain where you ascend, and be gathered to your people, as Aaron your brother died on Mount Hor and was gathered to his people, because you broke faith with Me in the midst of the sons of Israel at the waters of Meribah-kadesh, in the wilderness of Zin, because you did not treat Me as holy in the midst of the sons of Israel. For you shall see the land at a distance, but you shall not go there, into the land which I am giving the sons of Israel."

Joshua 2:1-14 Then Joshua the son of Nun sent two men as spies secretly from Shittim, saying, "Go, view the land, especially **Jericho**." So they went and came into the house of a harlot whose name was Rahab, and lodged there. It was told the king of **Jericho**, saying, "Behold, men from the sons of Israel have come here tonight to search out the land." And the king of **Jericho** sent word to Rahab, saying, "Bring out

Todd Bolen/BiblePlaces.com

the men who have come to you, who have entered your house, for they have come to search out all the land." But the woman had taken the two men and hidden them, and she said, "Yes, the men came to me, but I did not know where they were from. It came about when it was time to shut the gate at dark, that the men went out; I do not know where the men went. Pursue them quickly, for you will overtake them." But she had brought them up to the roof and hidden them in the stalks of flax which she had laid in order on the roof. So the men pursued them on the road to the Jordan to the fords; and as soon as those who were pursuing them had gone out, they shut the gate. Now before they lay down, she came up to them on the roof, and said to the men, "I know that the Lord has given you the land, and that the terror of you has fallen on us, and that all the inhabitants of the land have melted away before you. For we have heard how the Lord dried up the water of the Red Sea before you when you came out of Egypt, and what you did to the two kings of the Amorites who were beyond the Jordan, to Sihon and Og, whom you utterly destroyed. When we heard it, our hearts melted and no courage remained in any man any longer because of you; for the Lord your God, He is God in heaven above and on earth beneath. Now therefore, please swear to me by the Lord, since I have dealt kindly with you, that you also will deal kindly with my father's household, and give me a pledge of truth, and spare my father and my mother and my brothers and my sisters, with all who belong to them, and deliver our lives from death." So the men said to her, "Our life for yours if you do not tell this business of ours; and it shall come about when the Lord gives us the land that we will deal kindly and faithfully with you."

Todd Bolen/BiblePlaces.com

Joshua 6:1-27 Now **Jericho** was tightly shut because of the sons of Israel; no one went out and no one came in. The Lord said to Joshua, "See, I have given **Jericho** into your hand, with its king and the valiant warriors. You shall march around the city, all the men of war circling the city once. You shall do so for six days. Also seven priests shall carry seven trumpets of rams' horns before the ark; then on the seventh day you shall march around the city seven times, and the priests shall blow the trumpets. It shall be that when they make a long blast with the ram's horn, and when you hear the sound of the trumpet, all the people shall shout with a great shout; and the wall of the city will fall down flat, and the people will go up every man straight ahead." So Joshua the son of Nun called the priests and said to them, "Take up the ark of the covenant, and let seven priests carry seven trumpets of rams' horns before the ark of the Lord." Then he said to the people, "Go forward, and march around the city, and let the armed men go on before the ark of the Lord." And it was so, that when Joshua had spoken to the people, the seven priests carrying the seven trumpets of rams' horns before the Lord went forward and blew the trumpets; and the ark of the covenant of the Lord followed them. The armed men went before the priests who blew the trumpets, and the rear guard came after the ark, while they continued to blow the trumpets. But Joshua commanded the people, saying, "You shall not shout nor let your voice be heard nor let a word proceed out of your mouth, until the day I tell you, 'Shout!' Then you shall shout!" So he had the ark of the Lord taken around the city, circling it once; then they came into the camp and spent the night in the camp. Now Joshua rose early in the morning, and the priests took up the ark of the Lord. The seven priests carrying the seven trumpets of rams' horns before the ark of the Lord went on continually, and blew the trumpets; and the armed men went before them and the rear guard came after the ark of the Lord, while they continued to blow the trumpets. Thus the second day they marched around the city once and returned to the camp; they did so for six days. Then on the seventh day they rose early at the dawning of the day and marched around the city in the same manner seven times; only on that day they marched around the city seven times. At the seventh time, when the priests blew the trumpets, Joshua said to the people, "Shout! For the Lord has given you the city. The city shall be under the ban, it and all that is in it belongs to the Lord; only Rahab the harlot and all who are with her in the house shall live, because she hid the messengers whom we sent. But as for you, only keep yourselves from the things under the ban, so that you do not covet them and take some of the things under the ban, and make the camp of Israel accursed and bring trouble on it. But all the silver and gold and articles of bronze and iron are holy to the Lord; they shall go into the treasury of the Lord." So the people shouted, and priests blew the trumpets; and when the people heard the sound of the trumpet, the people shouted with a great shout and the wall fell down flat, so that the people went up into the city, every man straight ahead, and they took the city. They utterly destroyed everything in the city, both man and woman, young and old, and ox and sheep and donkey, with the edge of the sword. Joshua said to the two men who had spied out the land, "Go into the harlot's house and bring the woman and all she has out of there, as you have sworn to her." So the young men who were spies went in and brought out Rahab and her father and her mother and her brothers and all she had; they also brought out all her relatives and placed them outside the camp of Israel. They burned the city with fire, and all that was in it. Only the silver and gold, and articles of bronze and iron, they put into the treasury of the house of the Lord. However, Rahab the harlot and her father's household and all she had, Joshua spared; and she has lived in the midst of Israel to this day, for she hid the messengers whom Joshua sent to spy out **Jericho**. Then Joshua made them take an oath at that time, saying, "Cursed before the Lord is the man who rises up and builds this city **Jericho**; with the loss of his firstborn he shall lay its foundation, and with the loss of his youngest son he shall set up its gates." So the Lord was with Joshua, and his fame was in all the land.

2 Samuel 10:1-5 Now it happened afterwards that the king of the Ammonites died, and Hanun his son became king in his place. Then David said, "I will show kindness to Hanun the son of Nahash, just as his father showed kindness to me." So David sent some of his servants to console him concerning his father. But when David's servants came to the land of the Ammonites, the princes of the Ammonites said to Hanun their lord, "Do you think that David is honoring your father because he has sent consolers to you? Has David not sent his servants to you in order to search the city, to spy it out and overthrow it?" So Hanun took David's servants and shaved off half of their beards, and cut off their garments in the middle as far as their hips, and sent them away. When they told it to David, he sent to meet them, for the men were greatly humiliated. And the king said, "Stay at **Jericho** until your beards grow, and then return."

1 Kings 16:31-34 It came about, as though it had been a trivial thing for him to walk in the sins of Jeroboam the son of Nebat, that he married Jezebel the daughter of Ethbaal king of the Sidonians, and went to serve Baal and worshiped him. So he erected an altar for Baal in the house of Baal which he built in Samaria. Ahab also made the Asherah. Thus Ahab did more to provoke the Lord God of Israel than all the kings of Israel who were before him. In his days Hiel the Bethelite

built **Jericho**; he laid its foundations with the loss of Abiram his firstborn, and set up its gates with the loss of his youngest son Segub, according to the word of the Lord, which He spoke by Joshua the son of Nun.

Matthew 20:29-34 As they were leaving **Jericho**, a large crowd followed Him. And two blind men sitting by the road, hearing that Jesus was passing by, cried out, "Lord, have mercy on us, Son of David!" The crowd sternly told them to be quiet, but they cried out all the more, "Lord, Son of David, have mercy on us!" And Jesus stopped and called them, and said, "What do you want Me to do for you?" They said to Him, "Lord, we want our eyes to be opened." Moved with compassion, Jesus touched their eyes; and immediately they regained their sight and followed Him.

Todd Bolen/BiblePlaces.com

Mark 10:46-52 Then they came to **Jericho**. And as He was leaving **Jericho** with His disciples and a large crowd, a blind beggar named Bartimaeus, the son of Timaeus, was sitting by the road. When he heard that it was Jesus the Nazarene, he began to cry out and say, "Jesus, Son of David, have mercy on me!" Many were sternly telling him to be quiet, but he kept crying out all the more, "Son of David, have mercy on me!" And Jesus stopped and said, "Call him here." So they called the blind man, saying to him, "Take courage, stand up! He is calling for you." Throwing aside his cloak, he jumped up and came to Jesus. And answering

Todd Bolen/BiblePlaces.com

him, Jesus said, "What do you want Me to do for you?" And the blind man said to Him, "Rabboni, I want to regain my sight!" And Jesus said to him, "Go; your faith has made you well." Immediately he regained his sight and began following Him on the road.

Todd Bolen/BiblePlaces.com

Luke 10:30-37 Jesus replied and said, "A man was going down from Jerusalem to **Jericho**, and fell among robbers, and they stripped him and beat him, and went away leaving him half dead. And by chance a priest was going down on that road, and when he saw him, he passed by on the other side. Likewise a Levite also, when he came to the place and saw him, passed by on the other side. But a Samaritan, who was on a journey, came upon him; and when he saw him, he felt compassion, and came to him and bandaged up his wounds, pouring oil and wine on them; and he put him on his own beast, and brought him to an inn and took care of him. On the next day he took out two denarii and gave them to the innkeeper and said, 'Take care of him; and whatever more you spend, when I return I will repay you.' Which of these three do you think proved to be a neighbor to the man who fell into the robbers' hands?" And he said, "The one who showed mercy toward him." Then Jesus said to him, "Go and do the same."

Luke 19:1-9 He entered **Jericho** and was passing through. And there was a man called by the name of Zaccheus; he was a chief tax collector and he was rich. Zaccheus was trying to see who Jesus was, and was unable because of the crowd, for he was small in stature. So he ran on ahead and climbed up into a sycamore tree in order to see Him, for He was about to pass through that way. When Jesus came to the place, He looked up and said to him, "Zaccheus, hurry and come down, for today I must stay at your house." And he hurried and came down and received Him gladly. When they saw it, they all began to grumble, saying, "He has gone to be the guest of a man who is a sinner." Zaccheus stopped and said to the Lord, "Behold, Lord, half of my possessions I will give to the poor, and if I have defrauded anyone of anything, I will give back four times as much." And Jesus said to him, "Today salvation has come to this house, because he, too, is a son of Abraham."

Hebrews 11:30-31 By faith the walls of **Jericho** fell down after they had been encircled for seven days. By faith Rahab the harlot did not perish along with those who were disobedient, after she had welcomed the spies in peace.

David Bivin/LifeintheHolyLand.com

JERUSALEM

Interesting Facts:

- *David reigned in Jerusalem.*
- *David had his affair with Bathsheba in Jerusalem.*
- *Solomon built the wall around Jerusalem.*
- *Solomon built the first temple in Jerusalem.*
- *The Queen of Sheba visited Solomon in Jerusalem.*
- *Mary and Joseph went each year to Jerusalem for the Passover.*
- *Jesus cleared the temple.*
- *Jesus was taken into custody, beaten, crucified and resurrected in and around Jerusalem.*
- *Paul persecuted Christians before he was saved in Jerusalem.*

---

2 Samuel 5:5-6 At Hebron he reigned over Judah seven years and six months, and in **Jerusalem** he reigned thirty-three years over all Israel and Judah. Now the king and his men went to **Jerusalem** against the Jebusites, the inhabitants of the land, and they said to David, "You shall not come in here, but the blind and lame will turn you away"; thinking, "David cannot enter here."

2 Samuel 11:1-15 Then it happened in the spring, at the time

Image on page 82
LC-DIG-ppmsca-02702/www.LifeintheHolyLand.com

Todd Bolen/BiblePlaces.com

when kings go out to battle, that David sent Joab and his servants with him and all Israel, and they destroyed the sons of Ammon and besieged Rabbah. But David stayed at **Jerusalem**. Now when evening came David arose from his bed and walked around on the roof of the king's house, and from the roof he saw a woman bathing; and the woman was very beautiful in appearance. So David sent and inquired about the woman. And one said, "Is this not Bathsheba, the daughter of Eliam, the wife of Uriah the Hittite?" David sent messengers and took her, and when she came to him, he lay with her; and when she had purified herself from her uncleanness, she returned to her house. The woman conceived; and she sent and told David, and said, "I am pregnant." Then David sent to Joab, saying, "Send me Uriah the Hittite." So Joab sent Uriah to David. When Uriah came to him, David asked concerning the welfare of Joab and the people and the state of the war. Then David said to Uriah, "Go down to your house, and wash your feet." And Uriah went out of the king's house, and a present from the king was sent out after him. But Uriah slept at the door of the king's house with all the servants of his lord, and did not go down to his house. Now when they told David, saying, "Uriah did not go down to his house," David said to Uriah, "Have you not come from a journey?

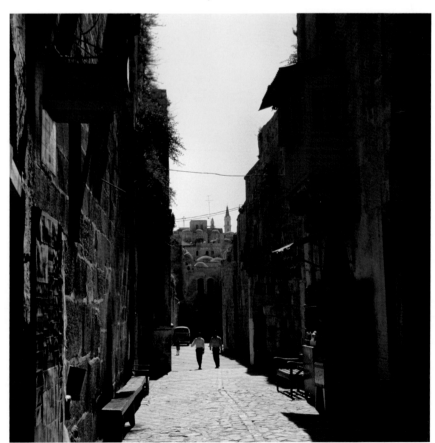

David Bivin/LifeintheHolyLand.com

Why did you not go down to your house?" Uriah said to David, "The ark and Israel and Judah are staying in temporary shelters, and my lord Joab and the servants of my lord are camping in the open field. Shall I then go to my house to eat and to drink and to lie with my wife? By your life and the life of your soul, I will not do this thing." Then David said to Uriah, "Stay here today also, and tomorrow I will let you go." So Uriah remained in **Jerusalem** that day and the next. Now David called him, and he ate and drank before him, and he made him drunk; and in the evening he went out to lie on his bed with his lord's servants, but he did not go down to his house. Now in the morning David wrote a letter to Joab and sent it by the hand of Uriah. He had written in the letter, saying, "Place Uriah in the front line of the fiercest battle and withdraw from him, so that he may be struck down and die."

Todd Bolen/BiblePlaces.com

1 Kings 3:1 Then Solomon formed a marriage alliance with Pharaoh king of Egypt, and took Pharaoh's daughter and brought her to the city of David until he had finished building his own house and the house of the Lord and the wall around **Jerusalem**.

1 Kings 9:15-19 Now this is the account of the forced labor which King Solomon levied to build the house of the Lord, his own house, the Millo, the wall of **Jerusalem**, Hazor, Megiddo, and Gezer. For Pharaoh king of Egypt had gone up and captured Gezer and burned it with fire, and killed the Canaanites who lived in the city, and had given it as a dowry to his daughter, Solomon's wife. So Solomon rebuilt Gezer and the lower Beth-horon and Baalath and Tamar in the wilderness, in the land of Judah, and all the storage cities which Solomon had, even the cities for his chariots and the cities for his horsemen, and all that it pleased Solomon to build in **Jerusalem**, in Lebanon, and in all the land under his rule.

Daniel Frese/BiblePlaces.com

1 Kings 10:1-2 Now when the queen of Sheba heard about the fame of Solomon concerning the name of the Lord, she came to test him with difficult questions. So she came to **Jerusalem** with a very large retinue, with camels carrying spices and very much gold and precious stones. When she came to Solomon, she spoke with him about all that was in her heart.

2 Chronicles 3:1 Then Solomon began to build the house of the Lord in **Jerusalem** on Mount Moriah, where the Lord had appeared to his father David, at the place that David had prepared on the threshing floor of Ornan the Jebusite.

Todd Bolen/BiblePlaces.com

Psalm 122:2 Our feet are standing Within your gates, O **Jerusalem**,…

Matthew 16:21 From that time Jesus began to show His disciples that He must go to **Jerusalem**, and suffer many things from the elders and chief priests and scribes, and be killed, and be raised up on the third day.

Matthew 20:17-18 As Jesus was about to go up to **Jerusalem**, He took the twelve disciples aside by themselves, and on the way He said to them, "Behold, we are going up to **Jerusalem**; and the Son of Man will be delivered to the chief priests and scribes, and they will condemn Him to death.

Matthew 21:10 When He had entered **Jerusalem**, all the city was stirred, saying, "Who is this?"

Mark 11:11-28 Jesus entered **Jerusalem** and came into the temple; and after looking around at everything, He left for Bethany with the twelve, since it was already late. On the next day, when they had left Bethany, He became hungry. Seeing at a distance a fig tree in leaf, He went to see if perhaps He would find anything on it; and when He came to it, He found nothing but leaves, for it was not the season for figs. He said to it, "May no one ever eat fruit from you again!" And His

Todd Bolen/BiblePlaces.com

disciples were listening. Then they came to **Jerusalem**. And He entered the temple and began to drive out those who were buying and selling in the temple, and overturned the tables of the money changers and the seats of those who were selling doves; and He would not permit anyone to carry merchandise through the temple. And He began to teach and say to them, "Is it not written, 'My house shall be called a house of prayer for all the nations'? But you have made it a robbers' den." The chief priests and the scribes heard this, and began seeking how to destroy Him; for they were afraid of Him, for the whole crowd was astonished at His teaching. When evening came, they would go out of the city. As they were passing by in the morning, they saw the fig tree withered from the roots up. Being reminded, Peter said to Him, "Rabbi, look, the fig tree which You cursed has withered." And Jesus answered saying to them, "Have faith in God. "Truly I say to you, whoever says to this mountain, 'Be taken up and cast into the sea,' and does not doubt in his heart, but believes that what he says is going to happen, it will be granted him. "Therefore I say to you, all things for which you pray and ask, believe that you have received them, and they will be granted you. Whenever you stand praying, forgive, if you have anything

Todd Bolen/BiblePlaces.com

against anyone, so that your Father who is in heaven will also forgive you your transgressions. ["But if you do not forgive, neither will your Father who is in heaven forgive your transgressions."] They came again to **Jerusalem**. And as He was walking in the temple, the chief priests and the scribes and the elders came to Him, and began saying to Him, "By what authority are You doing these things, or who gave You this authority to do these things?"

Luke 2:41 Now His parents went to **Jerusalem** every year at the Feast of the Passover.

Todd Bolen/BiblePlaces.com

Luke 13:33-34 "Nevertheless I must journey on today and tomorrow and the next day; for it cannot be that a prophet would perish outside of **Jerusalem**. O **Jerusalem**, **Jerusalem**, the city that kills the prophets and stones those sent to her! How often I wanted to gather your children together, just as a hen gathers her brood under her wings, and you would not have it!"

Acts 9:13-28 But Ananias answered, "Lord, I have heard from many about this man, how much harm he did to Your saints at **Jerusalem**; and here he has authority from the chief priests to bind all who call on Your name." But the Lord said to him, "Go, for he is a chosen instrument of Mine, to bear My name before the Gentiles and kings and the sons of

Israel; for I will show him how much he must suffer for My name's sake."
So Ananias departed and entered the house, and after laying his hands on

him said, "Brother Saul, the Lord Jesus, who appeared to you on the road by which you were coming, has sent me so that you may regain your sight and be filled with the Holy Spirit." And immediately there fell from his eyes something like scales, and he regained his sight, and he got up and was baptized; and he took food and was strengthened. Now for several days he was with the disciples who were at Damascus, and immediately he began to proclaim Jesus in

Todd Bolen/BiblePlaces.com

the synagogues, saying, "He is the Son of God." All those hearing him continued to be amazed, and were saying, "Is this not he who in **Jerusalem** destroyed those who called on this name, and who had come here for the purpose of bringing them bound before the chief priests?" But Saul kept increasing in strength and confounding the Jews who lived at Damascus by proving that this Jesus is the Christ. When many days had elapsed, the Jews plotted together to do away with him, but their plot became known to Saul. They were also watching the gates day and night so that they might put him to death; but his disciples took him by

Todd Bolen/BiblePlaces.com

night and let him down through an opening in the wall, lowering him in a large basket. When he came to **Jerusalem**, he was trying to associate with the disciples; but they were all afraid of him, not believing that he was a

LC-DIG-ppmsca-02700/www.LifeintheHolyLand.com

disciple. But Barnabas took hold of him and brought him to the apostles and described to them how he had seen the Lord on the road, and that He had talked to him, and how at Damascus he had spoken out boldly in the name of Jesus. And he was with them, moving about freely in **Jerusalem**, speaking out boldly in the name of the Lord.

Acts 20:22 "And now, behold, bound by the Spirit, I am on my way to **Jerusalem**, not knowing what will happen to me there.

Todd Bolen/BiblePlaces.com

JORDAN RIVER

Interesting Facts:

- *John the Baptist baptized people in the Jordan River.*

- *Jesus was baptized in the Jordan River.*

Matthew 3:5-6 Then Jerusalem was going out to him, and all Judea and all the district around the Jordan; and they were being baptized by him in the **Jordan River**, as they confessed their sins.

Matthew 3:13 Then Jesus arrived from Galilee at the **Jordan** coming to John, to be baptized by him.

Mark 1:5-9 And all the country of Judea was going out to him, and all the people of Jerusalem; and they were being baptized by him in the **Jordan River**, confessing their sins. John was clothed with camel's hair and wore a leather belt around his waist, and his diet was locusts and wild honey. And he was preaching, and saying, "After me One is coming who is mightier than I, and I am not fit to stoop down and untie the thong of His sandals. I baptized you with water; but He will baptize you with the Holy Spirit." In those days Jesus came from Nazareth in Galilee and was baptized by John in the **Jordan**.

Todd Bolen/BiblePlaces.com
Image on page 92 - Todd Bolen/BiblePlaces.com

Todd Bolen/BiblePlaces.com

John 10:40 And He went away again beyond the **Jordan** to the place where John was first baptizing, and He was staying there.

15,052. P. Z - LE COURS DU JOURDAIN, LIEU DU BAPTÊME.

LC-DIG-ppmsca-02717/www.LifeintheHolyLand.com

Todd Bolen/BiblePlaces.com

Todd Bolen/BiblePlaces.com

MEGIDDO

Interesting Facts:

- *Megiddo was originally a Canaanite city and the tribe of Manasseh did not completely control it when given their portion of land.*

- *Solomon fortified Megiddo and made it a stronghold.*

- *King Ahaziah died in Megiddo.*

- *King Josiah was killed in Megiddo.*

- *It is assumed by many that Megiddo will be the place of the "final battle".*

- *In Revelation it says the Euphrates River will dry up and make way for the Kings of the East and they will gather at Har-Magaedan which is Hebrew for Mount Megiddo.*

Judges 1:27 But Manasseh did not take possession of Beth-shean and its villages, or Taanach and its villages, or the inhabitants of Dor and its villages, or the inhabitants of Ibleam and its villages, or the inhabitants of **Megiddo** and its villages; so the Canaanites persisted

Todd Bolen/BiblePlaces.com
Image on page 96 - Todd Bolen/BiblePlaces.com

in living in that land.

Todd Bolen/BiblePlaces.com

1 Kings 9:15 Now this is the account of the forced labor which King Solomon levied to build the house of the Lord, his own house, the Millo, the wall of Jerusalem, Hazor, **Megiddo**, and Gezer.

2 Kings 9:27 When Ahaziah the king of Judah saw this, he fled by the way of the garden house. And Jehu pursued him and said, "Shoot him too, in the chariot." So they shot him at the ascent of Gur, which is at Ibleam. But he fled to **Megiddo** and died there.

Todd Bolen/BiblePlaces.com

2 Kings 23:29-30 In his days Pharaoh Neco king of Egypt went up to the king of Assyria to the river Euphrates. And King Josiah went to meet him, and when Pharaoh Neco saw him he killed him at **Megiddo**. His servants drove his body in a chariot from **Megiddo**, and brought him to Jerusalem and buried him in his own tomb. Then the people of the land took Jehoahaz the son of Josiah and anointed him and made him king in place of his father.

1 Chronicles 7:29 and along the borders of the sons of Manasseh, Beth-shean with its towns, Taanach with its towns, **Megiddo** with its towns, Dor with its towns. In these lived the sons of Joseph the son of Israel.

2 Chronicles 35:22 However, Josiah would not turn away from him, but disguised himself in order to make war with him; nor did he listen to the

words of Neco from the mouth of God, but came to make war on the plain of **Megiddo**.

Zechariah 12:11 "In that day there will be great mourning in Jerusalem, like the mourning of Hadadrimmon in the plain of **Megiddo**."

Revelation 16:12-16 The sixth angel poured out his bowl on the great river, the Euphrates; and its water was dried up, so that the way would be prepared for the kings from the east. And I saw coming out of the mouth of the dragon and out of the mouth of the beast and out of the mouth of the false prophet, three unclean spirits like frogs; for they are spirits of demons, performing signs, which go out to the kings of the whole world, to gather them together for the war of the great day of God, the Almighty. ("Behold, I am coming like a thief. Blessed is the one who stays awake and keeps his clothes, so that he will not walk about naked and men will not see his shame.") And they gathered them together to the place which in Hebrew is called Har-Magedon. (Har-Magaedon is the Hebrew name for Mt. **Megiddo**)

Todd Bolen/BiblePlaces.com

Todd Bolen/BiblePlaces.com

Todd Bolen/BiblePlaces.com

MOUNT CARMEL

Interesting Facts:

- *Mount Carmel is on the coast of the Mediterranean Sea and overlooks modern day Haifa.*

- *Mount Carmel is where is where Elijah and Ahab had a contest to see who was really God.*

- *Elijah killed all the prophets of Baal after God was proven to be God.*

- *Elijah prayed seven times on top of Mount Carmel for rain and waited to see as a distant cloud showed up.*

- *Elisha was at Mount Carmel when the Shunammite woman came to him because her son had died.*

1 Kings 18:17-40 When Ahab saw Elijah, Ahab said to him, "Is this you, you troubler of Israel?" He said, "I have not troubled Israel, but you and your father's house have, because you have forsaken the commandments of the Lord

Todd Bolen/BiblePlaces.com
Image on page 100 - Todd Bolen/BiblePlaces.com

and you have followed the Baals. Now then send and gather to me all Israel at **Mount Carmel**, together with 450 prophets of Baal and 400 prophets of the Asherah, who eat at Jezebel's table." So Ahab sent a message among all the sons of Israel and brought the prophets together at **Mount Carmel**. Elijah came near to all the people and said, "How long will you hesitate between two opinions? If the Lord is God, follow Him; but if Baal, follow him." But the people did not answer him a word. Then Elijah said to the people, "I alone am left a prophet of the Lord, but Baal's prophets are 450 men. Now let them give us two oxen; and let them choose one ox for themselves and cut it up, and place it on the wood, but put no fire under it; and I will prepare the other ox and lay it on the wood, and I will not put a fire under it. Then you call on the name of your god, and I will call on the name of the Lord, and the God who answers by fire, He is God." And all the people said, "That is a good idea." So Elijah said to the prophets of Baal, "Choose one ox for yourselves and prepare it first for you are many, and call on the name of your god, but put no fire under it." Then they took the ox which was given them and they prepared it and called on the name of Baal from morning until noon saying, "O Baal, answer us." But there was no voice and no one answered. And they leaped about the altar which they made. It came about at noon, that Elijah mocked them and said, "Call out with a loud voice, for he is a god; either he is occupied or gone aside, or is on a journey, or perhaps he is asleep and needs to be awakened." So they cried with a loud voice and cut themselves according to their custom with swords and lances until the blood gushed out on them. When midday was past, they raved until the time of the offering of the evening sacrifice; but there was no voice, no one answered, and no one paid attention. Then Elijah said to all the people, "Come near to me." So all the people came near to him. And he repaired the altar of the Lord which had been torn down. Elijah took twelve stones according to the number of the tribes of the sons of Jacob, to whom the word of the Lord had come, saying, "Israel shall be your name." So with the

stones he built an altar in the name of the Lord, and he made a trench around the altar, large enough to hold two measures of seed. Then he arranged the wood and cut the ox in pieces and laid it on the wood. And he said, "Fill four pitchers with water and pour it on the burnt offering and on the wood." And he said, "Do it a second time," and they did it a second time. And he said, "Do it a third time," and they

Todd Bolen/BiblePlaces.com

did it a third time. The water flowed around the altar and he also filled the trench with water. At the time of the offering of the evening sacrifice, Elijah the prophet came near and said, "O Lord, the God of Abraham, Isaac and

Israel, today let it be known that You are God in Israel and that I am Your servant and I have done all these things at Your word. Answer me, O Lord, answer me, that this people may know that You, O Lord, are God, and that You have turned their heart back again." Then the fire of the Lord fell and consumed the burnt offering and the wood and the stones and the dust, and licked up the water that was in the trench. When all the people saw it, they fell on their faces; and they said, "The

Todd Bolen/BiblePlaces.com

Lord, He is God; the Lord, He is God." Then Elijah said to them, "Seize the prophets of Baal; do not let one of them escape." So they seized them; and Elijah brought them down to the brook Kishon, and slew them there.

1 Kings 18:41-46 Now Elijah said to Ahab, "Go up, eat and drink; for there is the sound of the roar of a heavy shower." So Ahab went up to eat and drink. But Elijah went up to the top of **Carmel**; and he crouched down on the earth and put his face between his knees. He said to his servant, "Go up now, look toward the sea." So he went up and looked and said, "There is nothing." And he said, "Go back" seven times. It came about at the seventh time, that he said, "Behold, a cloud as small as a man's hand is coming up from the sea." And he said, "Go up, say to Ahab, 'Prepare your chariot and go down, so that the heavy shower does not stop you.' " In a little while the sky grew black with clouds and wind, and there was a heavy shower. And Ahab rode and went to Jezreel. Then the hand of the Lord was on Elijah, and he girded up his loins and outran Ahab to Jezreel.

Todd Bolen/BiblePlaces.com

2 Kings 2:25 He (*Elisha*) went from there to **Mount Carmel**, and from there he returned to Samaria. (Italics ours)

2 Kings 4:18-36 When the child was grown, the day came that he went out to his father to the reapers. He said to his father, "My head, my head." And he said to his servant, "Carry him to his mother." When he had taken him and brought him to his mother, he sat on her lap until noon, and then died. She went up and laid him on the bed of the man of God, and shut the door behind him and went out. Then she called to her husband and said, "Please send me one of the servants and one of the donkeys, that I may run to the man of God and return." He said, "Why will you go to him today? It is neither new moon nor sabbath." And she said, "It will be well." Then she saddled a donkey and said to her servant, "Drive and go forward; do not slow down the pace for me unless I tell you." So she went and came to the man of God to **Mount Carmel**. When the man of God saw her at a distance, he said to Gehazi his servant, "Behold, there is the Shunammite. Please run now to meet her

and say to her, 'Is it well with you? Is it well with your husband? Is it well with the child?' " And she answered, "It is well." When she came to the man of God to the hill, she caught hold of his feet. And Gehazi came near to push her away; but the man of God said, "Let her alone, for her soul is troubled within her; and the Lord has hidden it from me and has not told me." Then she said, "Did I ask for a son from my lord? Did I not say, 'Do not deceive me'?" Then he said to

Todd Bolen/BiblePlaces.com

Gehazi, "Gird up your loins and take my staff in your hand, and go your way; if you meet any man, do not salute him, and if anyone salutes you, do not answer him; and lay my staff on the lad's face." The mother of the lad said, "As the Lord lives and as you yourself live, I will not leave you." And he arose and followed her. Then Gehazi passed on before them and laid the staff on the lad's face, but there was no sound or response. So he returned to meet him and told him, "The lad has not awakened." When Elisha came into the house, behold the lad was dead and laid on his bed. So he entered and shut the door behind them both and prayed to the Lord. And he went up and lay on the child, and put his mouth on his mouth and his eyes on his eyes and his hands on his hands, and he stretched himself on him; and the flesh of the child became warm. Then he returned and walked in the house once back and forth, and went up and stretched himself on him; and the lad sneezed seven times and the lad opened his eyes. He called Gehazi and said, "Call this Shunammite." So he called her. And when she came in to him, he said, "Take up your son."

MOUNT OF BEATITUDES

Interesting Facts:

• *This mountain overlooks the Sea of Galilee.*

• *This is where Jesus taught the crowds "Blessed are the poor in spirit".*

Matthew 5:1-12 When Jesus saw the crowds, He went up on the mountain; and after He sat down, His disciples came to Him. He opened His mouth and began to teach them, saying, "Blessed are the poor in spirit, for theirs is the kingdom of heaven. Blessed are those who mourn, for they shall be comforted. Blessed are the gentle, for they shall inherit the earth. Blessed are those who hunger and thirst for righteousness, for they shall be satisfied. Blessed are the merciful, for they shall receive mercy. Blessed are the pure in heart, for they shall see God. Blessed are the peacemakers, for they shall be called sons of God. Blessed are those who have been persecuted for the sake of righteousness, for theirs is the kingdom of heaven. Blessed are you when people insult you and persecute you, and falsely say all kinds of evil against you because of Me. Rejoice and be glad, for your reward in heaven is great; for in the same way they persecuted the prophets who were before you.

Todd Bolen/BiblePlaces.com
Image on page 106 - Todd Bolen/BiblePlaces.com

MOUNT OF OLIVES

Interesting Facts:

- *The Mount of Olives is the hill which faces the Old City of Jerusalem on the Eastern side of the Kidron Valley.*

- *The Mount of Olives overlooks the Temple Mount.*

- *David wept and prayed on the Mount of Olives when his son Absalom took over his position of king.*

- *When Jesus returns, He will stand on the Mount of Olives and it will be split in two.*

- *Jesus was sitting on the Mount of Olives when his disciples asked Him about the end times.*

- *Jesus rode a donkey from the Mount of Olives into the City.*

- *After breaking bread in the upper room, Jesus and his disciples went to the Mount of Olives before Jesus was arrested and crucified.*

- *The Garden of Gethsamane is on the Mount of Olives.*

- *Jesus ascended to heaven from the Mount of Olives.*

Image on page 108
Todd Bolen/BiblePlaces.com

Todd Bolen/BiblePlaces.com

2 Samuel 15:30-37 And David went up the ascent of the **Mount of Olives**, and wept as he went, and his head was covered and he walked barefoot. Then all the people who were with him each covered his head and went up weeping as they went. Now someone told David, saying, "Ahithophel is among the conspirators with Absalom." And David said, "O Lord, I pray, make the counsel of Ahithophel foolishness." It happened as David was coming to the summit, where God was worshiped, that behold, Hushai the Archite met him with his coat torn and dust on his head. David said to him, "If you pass over with me, then you will be a burden to me. But if you return to the city, and say to Absalom, 'I will be your servant, O king; as I have been your father's servant in time past, so I will now be your servant,' then you can thwart the counsel of Ahithophel for me. Are not Zadok and Abiathar the priests with you there? So it shall be that whatever you hear from the king's house, you shall report to Zadok and Abiathar the priests.

Behold their two sons are with them there, Ahimaaz, Zadok's son and Jonathan, Abiathar's son; and by them you shall send me everything that you hear." So Hushai, David's friend, came into the city, and Absalom came into Jerusalem.

Zechariah 14:1-11 Behold, a day is coming for the Lord when the spoil taken from you will be divided among you. For I will gather all the nations against Jerusalem to battle,

Todd Bolen/BiblePlaces.com

and the city will be captured, the houses plundered, the women ravished and half of the city exiled, but the rest of the people will not be cut off from the city. Then the Lord will go forth and fight against those nations, as when He fights on a day of battle. In that day His feet will stand on the **Mount of Olives**, which is in front of Jerusalem on the east; and the **Mount of Olives** will be split in its middle from east to west by a very large valley, so that half of the mountain will move toward the north and the other half toward the south. You will flee by the valley of My mountains, for the valley of the mountains will reach to Azel; yes, you will flee just as you fled before the earthquake in the days of Uzziah king of Judah. Then the Lord, my God, will come, and all the holy ones with Him! In that day there will be no light; the luminaries will dwindle. For it will be a unique day which is known to the Lord, neither day nor night, but it will come about that at evening time there will be light. And in that day living waters will flow out of Jerusalem, half of them toward the eastern sea and the other half toward the western sea; it will be in summer as well as in winter. And the Lord will be king over all the earth; in that day the Lord will be the only one, and His name the only one. All the land will be changed into a plain from Geba to Rimmon south of Jerusalem; but Jerusalem will rise and remain on its site from Benjamin's Gate as far as the place of the First Gate to the Corner Gate, and from the Tower of Hananel to the king's wine presses. People will live in it, and there will no longer be a curse, for Jerusalem will dwell in security.

Matthew 21:1-11 When they had approached Jerusalem and had come to Bethphage, at the **Mount of Olives**, then Jesus sent two disciples, saying to them, "Go into the village opposite you, and immediately you will find a donkey tied there and a colt with her; untie them and bring them to Me. If anyone says anything to you, you

Todd Bolen/BiblePlaces.com

shall say, 'The Lord has need of them,' and immediately he will send them."
This took place to fulfill what was spoken through the prophet: "Say to the
daughter of Zion, 'Behold your King is coming to you, Gentle, and mounted
on a donkey, Even on a colt, the foal of a beast of burden.' " The disciples
went and did just as Jesus had instructed them, and brought the donkey
and the colt, and laid their coats on them; and He sat on the coats. Most of
the crowd spread their coats in the road, and others were cutting branches
from the trees and spreading them in the road. The crowds going ahead
of Him, and those who followed, were shouting, "Hosanna to the Son of
David; blessed is He who comes in the name of the Lord; Hosanna in the
highest!" When He had entered Jerusalem, all the city was stirred, saying,
"Who is this?" And the crowds were saying, "This is the prophet Jesus, from
Nazareth in Galilee."

Matthew 24:1-14 Jesus came out from the temple and was going away

Todd Bolen/BiblePlaces.com

when His disciples came up to
point out the temple buildings to
Him. And He said to them, "Do you
not see all these things? Truly I say
to you, not one stone here will be
left upon another, which will not be
torn down." As He was sitting on
the **Mount of Olives**, the disciples
came to Him privately, saying,
"Tell us, when will these things
happen, and what will be the sign
of Your coming, and of the end of
the age?" And Jesus answered and
said to them, "See to it that no one
misleads you. For many will come in My name, saying, 'I am the Christ,'
and will mislead many. You will be hearing of wars and rumors of wars.
See that you are not frightened, for those things must take place, but that
is not yet the end. For nation will rise against nation, and kingdom against
kingdom, and in various places there will be famines and earthquakes.
But all these things are merely the beginning of birth pangs. Then they will

deliver you to tribulation, and will kill you, and you will be hated by all nations because of My name. At that time many will fall away and will betray one another and hate one another. Many false prophets will arise and will mislead many. Because lawlessness is increased, most people's love will grow cold. But the one who endures to the end, he will be saved. This gospel of the kingdom shall be preached in the whole world as a testimony to all the nations, and then the end will come."

Matthew 26:26-35 While they were eating, Jesus took some bread, and after a blessing, He broke it and gave it to the disciples, and said, "Take, eat; this is My body." And when He had taken a cup and given thanks, He gave it to them, saying, "Drink from it, all of you; for this is My blood of the covenant, which is poured out for many for forgiveness of sins. But I say to you, I will not drink of this fruit of the vine from now on until that day when I drink it new with

Todd Bolen/BiblePlaces.com

you in My Father's kingdom." After singing a hymn, they went out to the **Mount of Olives**. Then Jesus said to them, "You will all fall away because of Me this night, for it is written, 'I will strike down the shepherd, and the sheep of the flock shall be scattered.' But after I have been raised, I will go ahead of you to Galilee." But Peter said to Him, "Even though all may fall away because of You, I will never fall away." Jesus said to him, "Truly I say to you that this very night, before a rooster crows, you will deny Me three times." Peter said to Him, "Even if I have to die with You, I will not deny You." All the disciples said the same thing too.

Luke 19:33-44 As they were untying the colt, its owners said to them, "Why are you untying the colt?" They said, "The Lord has need of it." They brought it to Jesus, and they threw their coats on the colt and put Jesus

on it. As He was going, they were spreading their coats on the road. As soon as He was approaching, near the descent of the **Mount of Olives**, the whole crowd of the disciples began to praise God joyfully with a loud voice for all the miracles which they had seen, shouting: "Blessed is the King who comes in the name of the Lord; Peace in heaven and glory in the highest!" Some of the Pharisees in the crowd said to Him, "Teacher, rebuke Your disciples." But Jesus answered, "I tell you, if these become silent, the stones will cry out!" When He approached Jerusalem, He saw the city and wept over it, saying, "If you had known in this day, even you, the things which make for peace! But now they have been hidden from your eyes. For the days will come upon you when your enemies will throw up a barricade against you, and surround you and hem you in on every side, and they will level you to the ground and your children within you, and they will not leave in you one stone upon another, because you did not recognize the time of your visitation."

Luke 22:39-46 And He came out and proceeded as was His custom to the **Mount of Olives**; and the disciples also followed Him. When He arrived at the place, He said to them, "Pray that you may not enter into temptation." And He withdrew from them about a stone's throw, and He knelt down and began to pray, saying, "Father, if You are willing, remove this cup from Me; yet not My will, but Yours be done." Now an angel from heaven appeared to Him, strengthening Him. And being in agony He was praying very fervently; and His sweat became like drops of blood, falling down upon the ground. When He rose from prayer, He came to the disciples and found them sleeping from sorrow, and said to them, "Why are you sleeping? Get up and pray that you may not enter into temptation."

John 8:1-11 But Jesus went to the **Mount of Olives**. Early in the morning

He came again into the temple, and all the people were coming to Him; and He sat down and began to teach them. The scribes and the Pharisees brought a woman caught in adultery, and having set her in the center of the court, they said to Him, "Teacher, this woman has been caught in adultery, in the very act. Now in the Law Moses commanded us to stone such women; what then do You say?"

They were saying this, testing Him, so that they might have grounds for accusing Him. But Jesus stooped down and with His finger wrote on the ground. But when they persisted in asking Him, He straightened up, and said to them, "He who is without sin among you, let him be the first to throw a stone at her." Again He stooped down and wrote on the ground. When they heard it, they began to go out one by one, beginning with the older ones, and He was left alone, and the woman, where she was, in the center of the court. Straightening up, Jesus said to her, "Woman, where are they? Did no one condemn you?" She said, "No one, Lord." And Jesus said, "I do not condemn you, either. Go. From now on sin no more."

Acts 1:9-14 And after He had said these things, He was lifted up while they were looking on, and a cloud received Him out of their sight. And as they were gazing intently into the sky while He was going, behold, two men in white clothing stood beside them. They also said, "Men of Galilee, why do you stand looking into the sky? This Jesus, who has been taken up from you into heaven, will come in just the same way as you have watched Him go into heaven." Then they returned to Jerusalem from the **mount called Olivet**, which is near Jerusalem, a Sabbath day's journey away. When they had entered the city, they went up to the upper room where they were staying; that is, Peter and John and James and Andrew, Philip and Thomas, Bartholomew and Matthew, James the son of Alphaeus, and Simon the Zealot, and Judas the son of James. These all with one mind were continually devoting themselves to prayer, along with the women, and Mary the mother of Jesus, and with His brothers.

Todd Bolen/BiblePlaces.com

Todd Bolen/BiblePlaces.com

NAZARETH

Interesting Facts:

- *An Angel came to Mary in Nazareth announcing she would conceive a Son by the Holy Spirit.*

- *Joseph was warned by God in a dream and took Jesus to Nazareth which is where they lived.*

- *Jesus was in the synagogue in Nazareth when He read Isaiah saying "Today the scripture has been fulfilled".*

Matthew 2:19-23 But when Herod died, behold, an angel of the Lord appeared in a dream to Joseph in Egypt, and said, "Get up, take the Child and His mother, and go into the land of Israel; for those who sought the Child's life are dead." So Joseph got up, took the Child and His mother, and came into the land of Israel.

But when he heard that Archelaus was reigning over Judea in place of his father Herod, he was afraid to go there. Then after being warned by God in a dream, he left for the regions of Galilee, and came and lived in a city called **Nazareth**. This was to fulfill what was spoken through the prophets: "He shall be called a Nazarene."

Matthew 21:10-11 When He had entered Jerusalem, all the city was stirred, saying, "Who is this?" And

Todd Bolen/BiblePlaces.com
Image on page 118 - Todd Bolen/BiblePlaces.com

the crowds were saying, "This is the prophet Jesus, from **Nazareth** in Galilee."

Todd Bolen/BiblePlaces.com

Mark 1:9 In those days Jesus came from **Nazareth** in Galilee and was baptized by John in the Jordan.

Luke 1:26-38 Now in the sixth month the angel Gabriel was sent from God to a city in Galilee called **Nazareth**, to a virgin engaged to a man whose name was Joseph, of the descendants of David; and the virgin's name was Mary. And coming in, he said to her, "Greetings, favored one! The Lord is with you." But she was very perplexed at this statement, and kept pondering what kind of salutation this was. The angel said to her, "Do not be afraid, Mary; for you have found favor with God. And behold, you will conceive in your womb and bear a son, and you shall name Him Jesus. He will be great and will be called the Son of the Most High; and the Lord God will give Him the throne of His father David;

LC-DIG-ppmsca-02730/www.LifeintheHolyLand.com

and He will reign over the house of Jacob forever, and His kingdom will have no end." Mary said to the angel, "How can this be, since I am a virgin?" The angel answered and said to her, "The Holy Spirit will come upon you, and the power of the Most High will overshadow you; and for that reason the holy Child shall be called the Son of God. And behold, even your relative Elizabeth has also conceived a son in her old age; and she who was called barren is now in her sixth month.

For nothing will be impossible with God." And Mary said, "Behold, the bondslave of the Lord; may it be done to me according to your word." And the angel departed from her.

Luke 2:1-7 Now in those days a decree went out from Caesar Augustus, that a census be taken of all the inhabited earth. This was the first census taken while Quirinius was governor of Syria. And everyone was on his way to register for the census, each to his own city. Joseph also went up from Galilee, from the city of **Nazareth**, to Judea, to the city of David which is called Bethlehem, because he was of the house and family of David, in order to register along with Mary, who was engaged to him, and was with child. While they were there, the days were completed for her to give birth. And she gave birth to her firstborn son; and she wrapped Him in cloths, and laid Him in a manger, because there was no room for them in the inn.

Todd Bolen/BiblePlaces.com

Luke 2:39-40 When they had performed everything according to the Law of the Lord, they returned to Galilee, to their own city of **Nazareth**. The Child continued to grow and become strong, increasing in wisdom; and the grace of God was upon Him.

David Bivin/LifeintheHolyLand.com

Luke 2:41-51 Now His parents went to Jerusalem every year at the Feast of the Passover. And when He became twelve, they went up there according to the custom of the Feast; and as they were returning, after spending the full number of days, the boy Jesus stayed behind in Jerusalem. But His parents were unaware of it, but supposed Him to be in the caravan, and went a day's journey; and they began looking for Him among their relatives and acquaintances. When they did not find Him, they returned to Jerusalem looking for Him. Then, after three days they found Him in the temple, sitting in the midst of the teachers, both listening to them and asking them questions. And all who heard Him were amazed at His understanding and His answers. When they saw Him, they were astonished; and His mother said to Him, "Son, why have You treated us this way? Behold, Your father and I have been anxiously looking for You." And He said to them, "Why is it that you were looking for Me? Did you not know that I had to be in My Father's house?" But they did not understand the statement which He had made to them. And He went down with them and came to **Nazareth**, and He continued in subjection to them; and His mother treasured all these things in her heart.

Luke 4:14-21 And Jesus returned to Galilee in the power of the Spirit, and news about Him spread through all the surrounding district. And He began teaching in their synagogues and was praised by all. And He came to **Nazareth**, where He had been brought up; and as was His custom, He entered the synagogue on the Sabbath, and stood up to read. And the book of the prophet Isaiah was handed to Him. And He opened the book and found the place where it was written, "The Spirit of the Lord is upon Me, because He anointed Me to preach the gospel to the poor. He has sent Me to proclaim release to the captives, and recovery of sight to the blind, to set free those who are oppressed, to proclaim the favorable year of the Lord." And He closed the book, gave it back to the attendant and sat down; and the eyes of all in the synagogue were fixed on Him. And He began to say to them, "Today this Scripture has been fulfilled in your hearing."

John 1:43-51 The next day He purposed to go into Galilee, and He found Philip. And Jesus said to him, "Follow Me." Now Philip was from Bethsaida, of the city of Andrew and Peter. Philip found Nathanael and said to him, "We have found Him of whom Moses in the Law and also the Prophets wrote—Jesus of **Nazareth**, the son of Joseph." Nathanael said to him, "Can any good thing come out of **Nazareth**?" Philip said to him, "Come and see." Jesus saw Nathanael coming to Him, and said of him, "Behold, an Israelite indeed, in whom there is no deceit!" Nathanael said to Him, "How do You know me?" Jesus answered and said to him, "Before Philip called you, when you were under the fig tree, I saw you." Nathanael answered Him, "Rabbi, You are the Son of God; You are the King of Israel." Jesus answered and said to him, "Because I said to you that I saw you under the fig tree, do you believe? You will see greater things than these." And He said to him, "Truly, truly, I say to you, you will see the heavens opened and the angels of God ascending and descending on the Son of Man."

POOL OF BETHESDA

Interesting Fact:

- *Jesus healed a man who had been sick for thirty eight years at the Pool of Bethesda.*

John 5:1-10 After these things there was a feast of the Jews, and Jesus went up to Jerusalem. Now there is in Jerusalem by the sheep gate a pool, which is called in Hebrew **Bethesda**, having five porticoes. In these lay a multitude of those who were sick, blind, lame, and withered, [waiting for the moving of the waters; for an angel of the Lord went down at certain seasons into the pool and stirred up the water; whoever then first, after the stirring up of the water, stepped in was made well from whatever disease with which he was afflicted.] A man was there who had been ill for thirty-eight years. When Jesus saw him lying there, and knew that he had already been a long time in that condition, He said to him, "Do you wish to get well?" The sick man answered Him, "Sir, I have no man to put me into the pool when the water is stirred up, but while I am coming, another steps down before me." Jesus said to him, "Get up, pick up your pallet and walk." Immediately the man became well, and picked up his pallet and began to walk. Now it was the Sabbath on that day. So the Jews were saying to the man who was cured, "It is the Sabbath, and it is not permissible for you to carry your pallet."

Todd Bolen/BiblePlaces.com
Image on page 124 - David Bivin/LifeintheHolyLand.com

POOL OF SILOAM

Interesting Fact:

• *Jesus told a blind man to go wash in the Pool of Siloam.*

John 9:5-14 "While I am in the world, I am the Light of the world." When He had said this, He spat on the ground, and made clay of the spittle, and applied the clay to his eyes, and said to him, "Go, wash in the **Pool of Siloam**" (which is translated, Sent). So he went away and washed, and came back seeing. Therefore the neighbors, and those who previously saw him as a beggar, were saying, "Is not this the one who used to sit and beg?" Others were saying, "This is he," still others were saying, "No, but he is like him." He kept saying, "I am the one." So they were saying to him, "How then were your eyes opened?" He answered, "The man who is called Jesus

made clay, and anointed my eyes, and said to me, 'Go to **Siloam** and wash'; so I went away and washed, and I received sight." They said to him, "Where is He?" He said, "I do not know." They brought to the Pharisees the man who was formerly blind. Now it was a Sabbath on the day when Jesus made the clay and opened his eyes.

SEA OF GALILEE
(Also called Sea of Tiberias)

Interesting Facts:

• *Jesus settled in Capernaum which is on the Sea of Galilee.*

• *Peter and Andrew were called to follow Jesus as they were casting their nets in the Sea of Galilee.*

• *Jesus walked on water in the Sea of Galilee.*

• *Jesus appeared to the disciples at the Sea of Galilee after He was resurrected.*

Isaiah 9:1-2 But there will be no more gloom for her who was in anguish; in earlier times He treated the land of Zebulun and the land of Naphtali with contempt, but later on He shall make it glorious, by the way of the **sea**, on the other side of Jordan, **Galilee** of the Gentiles. The people who walk in darkness will see a great light; Those who live in a dark land, The light will shine on them.

Matthew 4:12-17 Now when Jesus heard that John had been taken into custody, He withdrew into **Galilee**; and leaving Nazareth, He came and settled in Capernaum, which is by the **sea**, in the region of Zebulun and Naphtali. This was to fulfill what was spoken through Isaiah the prophet: "The land of Zebulun and the

land of Naphtali, By the way of the **sea**, beyond the Jordan, **Galilee** of the Gentiles— "The people who were sitting in darkness saw a great Light, and those who were sitting in the land and shadow of death, upon them a Light dawned." From that time Jesus began to preach and say, "Repent, for the kingdom of heaven is at hand."

Todd Bolen/BiblePlaces.com

Matthew 4:18-21 Now as Jesus was walking by the **Sea of Galilee**, He saw two brothers, Simon who was called Peter, and Andrew his brother, casting a net into the **sea**; for they were fishermen. And He said to them, "Follow Me, and I will make you fishers of men." Immediately they left their nets and followed Him. Going on from there He saw two other brothers, James the son of Zebedee, and John his brother, in the boat with Zebedee their father, mending their nets; and He called them.

Todd Bolen/BiblePlaces.com

Matthew 15:29-39 Departing from there, Jesus went along by the **Sea of Galilee**, and having gone up on the mountain, He was sitting there. And large crowds came to Him, bringing with them those who were lame, crippled, blind, mute, and many others, and they laid them down at His feet; and He healed them. So the crowd marveled as they saw the mute speaking, the crippled restored, and the lame walking, and the blind seeing; and they glorified the God of Israel. And Jesus called His disciples to Him, and said, "I feel compassion for the people, because they have remained with Me now three days and have nothing to eat; and I do not want to send them away hungry, for they might faint on the way." The disciples said to Him, "Where would we get so

many loaves in this desolate place to satisfy such a large crowd?" And Jesus said to them, "How many loaves do you have?" And they said, "Seven, and a few small fish." And He directed the people to sit down on the ground; and He took the seven loaves and the fish; and giving thanks, He broke them and started giving them to the disciples, and the disciples gave them to the people. And they all ate and were satisfied, and they picked up what was left over of the broken pieces,

Todd Bolen/BiblePlaces.com

seven large baskets full. And those who ate were four thousand men, besides women and children. And sending away the crowds, Jesus got

into the boat and came to the region of Magadan.

Mark 7:31-37 Again He went out from the region of Tyre, and came through Sidon to the **Sea of Galilee** within the region of Decapolis. They brought to Him one who was deaf and spoke with difficulty, and they implored Him to lay His hand on him. Jesus took him aside from the crowd, by himself, and put His fingers into his ears, and after spitting, He touched his tongue with the saliva; and looking

Todd Bolen/BiblePlaces.com

up to heaven with a deep sigh, He said to him, "Ephphatha!" that is, "Be opened!" And his ears were opened, and the impediment of his tongue was

removed, and he began speaking plainly. And He gave them orders not to tell anyone; but the more He ordered them, the more widely they continued to proclaim it. They were utterly astonished, saying, "He has done all things well; He makes even the deaf to hear and the mute to speak."

John 6:1-2 After these things Jesus went away to the other side of the **Sea of Galilee** (or Tiberias). A large crowd followed Him, because they saw the signs which He was performing on those who were sick.

Matthew 8:18-27 Now when Jesus saw a crowd around Him, He gave orders to depart to the other side of the **sea**. Then a scribe came and said to Him, "Teacher, I will follow You wherever You go." Jesus said to him, "The foxes have holes and the birds of the air have nests, but the Son of Man has nowhere to lay His head." Another of the disciples said to Him, "Lord, permit me first to go and bury my father." But Jesus said to him, "Follow Me, and allow the dead to bury their own dead." When He got into the boat, His disciples followed Him. And behold, there arose a great storm on the **sea**, so that the boat was being covered with the waves; but Jesus Himself was asleep. And they came to Him and woke Him, saying, "Save us, Lord; we are perishing!"

He said to them, "Why are you afraid, you men of little faith?" Then He got up and rebuked the winds and the **sea**, and it became perfectly calm. The men were amazed, and said, "What kind of a man is this, that even the winds and the **sea** obey Him?"

Matthew 9:1-8 Getting into a boat, Jesus crossed over the **sea** and came to His own city. And they brought to Him a paralytic lying on a bed.

Seeing their faith, Jesus said to the paralytic, "Take courage, son; your sins are forgiven." And some of the scribes said to themselves, "This fellow blasphemes." And Jesus knowing their thoughts said, "Why are you thinking evil in your hearts? "Which is easier, to say, 'Your sins are forgiven,' or to say, 'Get up, and walk'? "But so that you may know that the Son of Man has authority on earth to forgive sins"—then He said to the paralytic, "Get up, pick up your bed and go home." And he got up and went home. But when the crowds saw this, they were awestruck, and glorified God, who had given such authority to men.

Todd Bolen/BiblePlaces.com

Matthew 13:1-9 That day Jesus went out of the house and was sitting by the **sea**. And large crowds gathered to Him, so He got into a boat and sat down, and the whole crowd was standing on the beach. And He spoke many things to them in parables, saying, "Behold, the sower went out to sow; and as he

Todd Bolen/BiblePlaces.com

sowed, some seeds fell beside the road, and the birds came and ate them up. Others fell on the rocky places, where they did not have much soil; and immediately they sprang up, because they had no depth of soil. But when the sun had risen, they were scorched; and because they had no root, they withered away. Others fell among the thorns, and the thorns came up and choked them out. And others fell on the good soil and yielded a crop, some a hundredfold, some sixty, and some thirty. He who has ears, let him hear."

Matthew 16:5-12 And the disciples came to the other side of the **sea**, but they had forgotten to bring any bread. And Jesus said to them, "Watch out and beware of the leaven of the Pharisees and Sadducees." They began to

Todd Bolen/BiblePlaces.com

discuss this among themselves, saying, "He said that because we did not bring any bread." But Jesus, aware of this, said, "You men of little faith, why do you discuss among yourselves that you have no bread? Do you not yet understand or remember the five loaves of the five thousand, and how many baskets full you picked up? Or the seven loaves of the four thousand, and how many large baskets full you picked up? How is it that you do not understand that I did not speak to you concerning bread? But beware of the leaven of the Pharisees and Sadducees." Then they understood that He did not say to beware of the leaven of bread, but of the teaching of the Pharisees and Sadducees.

John 21:1-17 After these things Jesus manifested Himself again to the disciples at the **Sea of Tiberias**, and He manifested Himself in this way. Simon Peter, and Thomas called Didymus, and Nathanael of Cana in **Galilee**, and the sons of Zebedee, and two others of His disciples were together. Simon Peter said to them, "I am going fishing." They said to him, "We will also come with you." They went out and got into the boat; and that night they caught nothing. But when the day was now breaking, Jesus stood on the beach; yet the disciples did not know that it was Jesus. So Jesus said to them, "Children, you do not have any fish, do you?" They answered Him, "No." And He said to them, "Cast the net on the right-hand side of the boat and you will find a catch." So they cast, and then they were not able to haul it in because of the great number of fish. Therefore that disciple whom Jesus loved said to

David Bivin/LifeintheHolyLand.com

Peter, "It is the Lord." So when Simon Peter heard that it was the Lord, he put his outer garment on (for he was stripped for work), and threw himself into the **sea**. But the other disciples came in the little boat, for they were not far from the land, but about one hundred yards away, dragging the net full of fish. So when they got out on the land, they saw a charcoal fire already laid and fish placed on it, and bread. Jesus said to them, "Bring some of the fish which you have now caught." Simon Peter went up and drew the net to land, full of large fish, a hundred and fifty-three; and although there were so many, the net was not torn. Jesus said to them, "Come and have breakfast." None of the disciples ventured to question Him, "Who are You?" knowing that it was the Lord. Jesus came and took the bread and gave it to them, and the fish likewise. This is now the third time that Jesus was manifested to the disciples, after He was raised from the dead. So when they had finished breakfast, Jesus said to Simon Peter, "Simon, son of John, do you love Me more than these?" He said to Him, "Yes, Lord; You know that I love You." He said to him, "Tend My lambs." He said to him again a second time, "Simon, son of John, do you love Me?" He said to Him, "Yes, Lord; You know that I love You." He said to him, "Shepherd My sheep." He said to him the third time, "Simon, son of John, do you love Me?" Peter was grieved because He said to him the third time, "Do you love Me?" And he said to Him, "Lord, You know all things; You know that I love You." Jesus said to him, "Tend My sheep. (**Sea of Tiberias** is an alternate name for **Sea of Galilee**)

Todd Bolen/BiblePlaces.com

Todd Bolen/BiblePlaces.com

TEMPLE (Also known as Western Wall)

Interesting Facts:

- *Solomon built the first Temple.*

- *Solomon's Temple was destroyed by the Babylonians in 586BC.*

- *The Second Temple was rebuilt under Ezra and Nehimiah.*

- *The Third Temple was built by Herod.*

- *While Zachariah was serving in the Temple the Angel Gabriel told him he would have a son, John the Baptist.*

- *The Third Temple was the place where Jesus cleared out the moneychangers.*

- *Jesus told the disciples that the Temple would be destroyed and not one stone would stand on top of the other.*

- *Jesus was teaching in the Temple when the adulterous woman was brought to Him by the Pharisees.*

- *The Third Temple was destroyed in AD 70 by the Romans.*

- *The Islamic Dome on the Rock sits on this site as of today.*

Image on page 138 - David Bivin/LifeintheHolyLand.com

Todd Bolen/BiblePlaces.com

First **Temple**

1 Chronicles 29:1-19 Then King David said to the entire assembly, "My son Solomon, whom alone God has chosen, is still young and inexperienced and the work is great; for the **temple** is not for man, but for the Lord God. Now with all my ability I have provided for the house of my God the gold for the things of gold, and the silver for the things of silver, and the bronze for the things of bronze, the iron for the things of iron, and wood for the things of wood, onyx stones and inlaid stones, stones of antimony and stones of various colors, and all kinds of precious stones and alabaster in abundance. Moreover, in my delight in the house of my God, the treasure I have of gold and silver, I give to the house of my God, over and above all that I have already provided for the holy **temple**, namely, 3,000 talents of gold, of the gold of Ophir, and 7,000 talents of refined silver, to overlay the walls of the buildings; of gold for the things of gold and of silver for the things of silver, that is, for all the work done by the craftsmen. Who then is willing to consecrate himself this day to the Lord?" Then the rulers of the fathers' households, and the princes of the tribes of Israel, and the commanders of thousands and of hundreds, with the overseers over the king's work, offered willingly; and for the service for the house of God they gave 5,000 talents and 10,000 darics of gold, and 10,000 talents of silver, and 18,000 talents of brass, and 100,000 talents of iron. Whoever possessed precious stones gave them to the treasury

Todd Bolen/BiblePlaces.com

of the house of the Lord, in care of Jehiel the Gershonite. Then the people rejoiced because they had offered so willingly, for they made their offering to the Lord with a whole heart, and King David also rejoiced greatly. So David blessed the Lord in the sight of all the assembly; and David said, "Blessed are You, O Lord God of Israel our father, forever and ever. Yours, O Lord, is the greatness and the power and the glory and the victory and the majesty, indeed everything that is in the heavens and the earth; Yours is the dominion, O Lord, and You exalt Yourself as head over all. "Both riches and honor come from You, and You rule over all, and in Your hand is power and might; and it lies in Your hand to make great and to strengthen everyone. Now therefore, our God, we thank You, and praise Your glorious name. But who am I and who are my people that we should be able to offer as

Todd Bolen/BiblePlaces.com

generously as this? For all things come from You, and from Your hand we have given You. For we are sojourners before You, and tenants, as all our fathers were; our days on the earth are like a shadow, and there is no hope. O Lord our God, all this abundance that we have provided to build You a house for Your holy name, it is from Your hand, and all is Yours. Since I know, O my God, that You try the heart and delight in uprightness, I, in the integrity of my heart, have willingly offered all these things; so now with joy I have seen Your people, who are present here, make their offerings willingly to You. O Lord, the God of Abraham, Isaac and Israel, our fathers, preserve this forever in the intentions of the heart of Your people, and direct their heart to You; and give to my son Solomon a perfect heart to keep Your commandments, Your testimonies and Your statutes, and to do them all, and to build the **temple**, for which I have made provision."

2nd Rebuilt Temple

Ezra 3:9-14 Then Jeshua with his sons and brothers stood united with

Kadmiel and his sons, the sons of Judah and the sons of Henadad with their sons and brothers the Levites, to oversee the workmen in the **temple** of God. Now when the builders had laid the foundation of the **temple**

Todd Bolen/BiblePlaces.com

of the Lord, the priests stood in their apparel with trumpets, and the Levites, the sons of Asaph, with cymbals, to praise the Lord according to the directions of King David of Israel. They sang, praising and giving thanks to the Lord, saying, "For He is good, for His lovingkindness is upon Israel forever." And all the people shouted with a great shout when they praised the Lord because the foundation of the house of the

Lord was laid. Yet many of the priests and Levites and heads of fathers' households, the old men who had seen the first **temple**, wept with a loud voice when the foundation of this house was laid before their eyes, while many shouted aloud for joy, so that the people could not distinguish the sound of the shout of joy from the sound of the weeping of the people, for the people shouted with a loud shout, and the sound was heard far away.

3rd Temple that Herod Built and was destroyed by the Romans in AD70
Matthew 4:5-7 Then the devil took Him into the holy city and had Him stand on the pinnacle of the **temple**, and said to Him, "If You are the Son of God, throw Yourself down; for it is written, 'He will command His angels concerning You'; and 'On their hands they will bear You up, So that You will not strike Your foot against a stone.' " Jesus said to him, "On the other hand, it is written, 'You shall not put the Lord your God to the test.' "

Matthew 21:12-24 And Jesus entered the **temple** and drove out all those who were buying and selling in the **temple**, and overturned the tables of the money changers and the seats of those who were selling doves. And He said to them, "It is written, 'My house shall be called a house of prayer';

but you are making it a robbers' den." And the blind and the lame came to Him in the **temple**, and He healed them. But when the chief priests and the

scribes saw the wonderful things that He had done, and the children who were shouting in the **temple**, "Hosanna to the Son of David," they became indignant and said to Him, "Do You hear what these children are saying?" And Jesus said to them, "Yes; have you never read, 'Out of the mouth of infants and nursing babies You have prepared praise for Yourself'?" And He left them and went out of the city to Bethany, and spent the night there. Now in the morning, when He was

Todd Bolen/BiblePlaces.com

returning to the city, He became hungry. Seeing a lone fig tree by the road, He came to it and found nothing on it except leaves only; and He said to it, "No longer shall there ever be any fruit from you." And at once the

fig tree withered. Seeing this, the disciples were amazed and asked, "How did the fig tree wither all at once?" And Jesus answered and said to them, "Truly I say to you, if you have faith and do not doubt, you will not only do what was done to the fig tree, but even if you say to this mountain, 'Be taken up and cast into the sea,' it will happen. "And all things you ask in prayer, believing, you will receive." When He entered the **temple**, the chief priests and the elders of the people

Todd Bolen/BiblePlaces.com

came to Him while He was teaching, and said, "By what authority are You doing these things, and who gave You this authority?" Jesus said to them, "I will also ask you one thing, which if you tell Me, I will also tell you by what authority I do these things.

Matthew 24:1-3 Jesus came out from the **temple** and was going away when His disciples came up to point out the **temple** buildings to Him. And He said to them, "Do you not see all these things? Truly I say to you, not one stone here will be left upon another, which will not be torn down." As He was sitting on the Mount of Olives, the disciples came to Him privately, saying, "Tell us, when will these things happen, and what will be the sign of Your coming, and of the end of the age?"

Matthew 27:1-5 Now when morning came, all the chief priests and the elders of the people conferred together against Jesus to put Him to death; and they bound Him, and led Him away and delivered Him to Pilate the governor. Then when Judas, who had betrayed Him, saw that He had been condemned, he felt remorse and returned the thirty pieces of silver to the chief priests and elders, saying, "I have sinned by betraying innocent blood." But they said, "What is that to us? See to that yourself!" And he threw the pieces of silver into the **temple** sanctuary and departed; and he went away and hanged himself.

Matthew 27:50-51 And Jesus cried out again with a loud voice, and yielded up His spirit. And behold, the veil of the **temple** was torn in two from top to bottom; and the earth shook and the rocks were split.

Mark 13:1-4 As He was going out of the **temple**, one of His disciples said to Him, "Teacher, behold what wonderful stones and what wonderful buildings!" And Jesus said to him, "Do you see these great buildings? Not one stone will be left upon another which will not be torn down." As He was sitting on the Mount of Olives opposite the **temple**, Peter and James and John and Andrew were questioning Him privately, "Tell us, when will these things be, and what will be the sign when all these things are going to be fulfilled?"

Todd Bolen/BiblePlaces.com

Luke 1:7-9 But they had no child, because Elizabeth was barren, and they were both advanced in years. Now it happened that while he was performing his priestly service before God in the appointed order of his division, according to the custom of the priestly office, he was chosen by lot to enter the **temple** of the Lord and burn incense.

Luke 1:19-23 The angel answered and said to him, "I am Gabriel, who stands in the presence of God, and I have been sent to speak to you and to bring you this good news. And behold, you shall be silent and unable to speak until the day when these things take place, because you did not believe my words, which will be fulfilled in their proper time." The people were waiting for Zacharias, and

Todd Bolen/BiblePlaces.com

were wondering at his delay in the **temple**. But when he came out, he was unable to speak to them; and they realized that he had seen a vision in the **temple**; and he kept making signs to them, and remained mute. When the days of his priestly service were ended, he went back home.

Luke 22:52-53 Then Jesus said to the chief priests and officers of the **temple** and elders who had come against Him, "Have you come out with swords and clubs as you would against a robber? While I was with you daily in the **temple**, you did not lay hands on Me; but this hour and the power of darkness are yours."

Todd Bolen/BiblePlaces.com

John 2:14-21 And He found in the **temple** those who were selling oxen and sheep and doves, and the money changers seated at their tables. And He made a scourge of cords, and drove them all out of the **temple**, with the sheep and the oxen; and He poured out the coins of the money changers and overturned their tables; and to those who were selling the doves He said, "Take these things away; stop making My Father's house a place of business." His disciples remembered that it was written, "Zeal for Your house will consume me." The Jews then said to Him, "What sign do You show us as your authority for doing these things?" Jesus answered them, "Destroy this **temple**, and in three days I will raise it up." The Jews then said, "It took forty-six years to build this **temple**, and will You raise it up in three days?" But He was speaking of the **temple** of His body.

John 8:2-11 Early in the morning He came again into the **temple**, and all the people were coming to Him; and He sat down and began to teach them. The scribes and the Pharisees brought a woman caught in adultery, and having set her in the center of the court, they said to Him, "Teacher, this woman has been caught in adultery, in the very act. "Now in the Law Moses commanded us to stone such women; what then do You say?" They were saying this, testing Him, so that they might have grounds for accusing Him. But Jesus stooped down and with His finger wrote on the ground. But when they persisted in asking Him, He straightened up, and said to them, "He who is without sin among you, let him be the first to throw a stone at her." Again He stooped down and wrote on the ground. When they heard it, they began to go out one by one, beginning with the older ones, and He was left alone, and the woman, where she was, in the center of the court. Straightening up, Jesus said to her, "Woman, where are they? Did no one condemn you?" She said, "No one, Lord." And Jesus said, "I do not condemn you, either. Go. From now on sin no more."

Todd Bolen/BiblePlaces.com

Acts 3:1-8 Now Peter and John were going up to the **temple** at the ninth hour, the hour of prayer. And a man who had been lame from his mother's womb was being carried along, whom they used to set down every day at the gate of the **temple** which is called Beautiful, in order to beg alms of those who were entering the **temple**. When he saw Peter and John about to go into the **temple**, he began asking to receive alms. But Peter, along with John, fixed his gaze on him and said, "Look at us!" And he began to give them his attention, expecting to receive something from them. But Peter said, "I do not possess silver and gold, but what I do have I give to you: In the name of Jesus Christ the Nazarene—walk!" And seizing him by the right hand, he raised him up; and immediately his feet and his ankles were strengthened. With a leap he stood upright and began to walk; and he entered the **temple** with them, walking and leaping and praising God.

TOMB

Interesting Facts:

• *Joseph from Arimathea took the body of Jesus and laid it in his own new tomb.*

• *The stone had been rolled away from the tomb.*

• *The place where Jesus was crucified there was a garden, and in that garden a tomb.*

Matthew 27:57-61 When it was evening, there came a rich man from Arimathea, named Joseph, who himself had also become a disciple of Jesus. This man went to Pilate and asked for the body of Jesus. Then Pilate ordered it to be given to him. And Joseph took the body and wrapped it in a clean linen cloth, and laid it in his own new **tomb**, which he had hewn out in the rock; and he rolled a large stone against the entrance of the **tomb** and went away. And Mary Magdalene was there, and the other Mary, sitting opposite the grave.

Matthew 28:1-10 Now after the Sabbath, as it began to dawn toward the first day of the week, Mary Magdalene and the other Mary came to look at the grave. And behold, a severe earthquake had occurred, for an angel of the Lord descended from heaven and came and rolled away the stone and sat upon it. And his appearance was like lightning, and his clothing as

Todd Bolen/BiblePlaces.com
Image on page 148 - Todd Bolen/BiblePlaces.com

white as snow. The guards shook for fear of him and became like dead men. The angel said to the women, "Do not be afraid; for I know that you are looking for Jesus who has been crucified. He is not here, for He has risen, just as He said. Come, see the place where He was lying. Go quickly and tell His disciples that He has risen from the dead; and behold, He is going ahead of you into Galilee, there you will see Him; behold, I have told you." And they left the **tomb** quickly with fear and great joy and ran to report it to His disciples. And behold, Jesus met them and greeted them. And they came up and took hold of His feet and worshiped Him. Then Jesus said to them, "Do not be afraid; go and take word to My brethren to leave for Galilee, and there they will see Me."

Todd Bolen/BiblePlaces.com

Mark 15:42-47 When evening had already come, because it was the preparation day, that is, the day before the Sabbath, Joseph of Arimathea came, a prominent member of the Council, who himself was waiting for the kingdom of God; and he gathered up courage and went in before Pilate, and asked for the body of Jesus. Pilate wondered if He was dead by this time, and summoning the centurion, he questioned him as to whether He was already dead. And ascertaining this from the centurion, he granted the body to Joseph. Joseph bought a linen cloth, took Him down, wrapped Him in the linen cloth and laid Him in a **tomb** which had been hewn out in the rock; and he rolled a stone against the entrance of the **tomb**. Mary Magdalene and Mary the mother of Joses were looking on to see where He was laid.

Mark 16:1-8 When the Sabbath was over, Mary Magdalene, and Mary the mother of James, and Salome, bought spices, so that they might come and anoint Him. Very early on the first day of the week, they came to the **tomb** when the sun had risen. They were saying to one another, "Who will roll away the stone for us from the entrance of the **tomb**?" Looking up, they saw that the stone had been rolled away, although it was extremely large. Entering the **tomb**, they saw a young man sitting at the right, wearing a white robe; and they were amazed. And he said to them, "Do not be amazed; you are looking for Jesus the Nazarene, who has been crucified. He has risen; He is not here; behold, here is the place where they laid Him. But go, tell His disciples and Peter, 'He is going ahead of you to Galilee; there you will see Him, just as He told you.' " They went out and fled from the **tomb**, for trembling and astonishment had gripped them; and they said nothing to anyone, for they were afraid.

Todd Bolen/BiblePlaces.com

Luke 23:50-56 And a man named Joseph, who was a member of the Council, a good and righteous man (he had not consented to their plan and action), a man from Arimathea, a city of the Jews, who was waiting for the kingdom of God; this man went to Pilate and asked for the body of Jesus. And he took it down and wrapped it in a linen cloth, and laid Him in a **tomb** cut into the rock, where no one had ever lain. It was the preparation day, and the Sabbath was about to begin. Now the women who had come with Him out of Galilee followed, and saw the **tomb** and how His body was laid. Then they returned and prepared spices and perfumes. And on the Sabbath they rested according to the commandment.

Luke 24:1-12 But on the first day of the week, at early dawn, they came to the **tomb** bringing the spices which they had prepared. And they found the stone rolled away from the **tomb**, but when they entered, they did not find the body of the Lord Jesus. While they were perplexed about this, behold, two men suddenly stood near them in dazzling clothing; and as the women were terrified and bowed their faces to the ground, the men said to them, "Why do you seek the living One among the dead? He is not here, but He has risen. Remember how He spoke to you while He was still in Galilee, saying that the Son of Man must be delivered into the hands of sinful men, and be crucified, and the third day rise again." And they remembered His words, and returned from the **tomb** and reported all these things to the eleven and to all the rest. Now they were Mary Magdalene and Joanna and Mary the mother of James; also the other women with them were telling these things to the apostles. But these words appeared to them as nonsense, and they would not believe them. But Peter got up and ran to the **tomb**; stooping and looking in, he saw the linen wrappings only; and he went away to his home, marveling at what had happened.

John 19:38-42 After these things Joseph of Arimathea, being a disciple of Jesus, but a secret one for fear of the Jews, asked Pilate that he might take away the body of Jesus; and Pilate granted permission. So he came and took away His body. Nicodemus, who had first come to Him by night, also came, bringing a mixture of myrrh and aloes, about a hundred pounds weight. So they took the body of Jesus and bound it in linen wrappings with the spices, as is the burial custom of the Jews. Now in the place where He was crucified there was a garden, and in the garden a new **tomb** in which no one had yet been laid. Therefore because of the Jewish day of preparation, since the **tomb** was nearby, they laid Jesus there.

Todd Bolen/BiblePlaces.com

John 20:1-10 Now on the first day of the week Mary Magdalene came early to the **tomb**, while it was still dark, and saw the stone already taken away from the **tomb**. So she ran and came to Simon Peter and to the other disciple whom Jesus loved, and said to them, "They have taken away the Lord out of the **tomb**, and we do not know where they have laid Him." So Peter and the other disciple went forth, and they were going to the **tomb**. The two were running together; and the other disciple ran ahead faster than Peter and came to the **tomb** first; and stooping and looking in, he saw the linen wrappings lying there; but he did not go in. And so Simon Peter also came, following him, and entered the **tomb**; and he saw the linen wrappings lying there, and the face-cloth which had been on His head, not lying with the linen wrappings, but rolled up in a place by itself. So the other disciple who had first come to the **tomb** then also entered, and he saw and believed. For as yet they did not understand the Scripture, that He must rise again from the dead. So the disciples went away again to their own homes.

John 20:11-18 But Mary was standing outside the **tomb** weeping; and so, as she wept, she stooped and looked into the **tomb**; and she saw two angels in white sitting, one at the head and one at the feet, where the body of Jesus had been lying. And they said to her, "Woman, why are you weeping?" She said to them, "Because they have taken away my Lord, and I do not know where they have laid Him." When she had said this, she turned around and saw Jesus standing there, and did not know that it was Jesus. Jesus said to her, "Woman, why are you weeping? Whom are you seeking?" Supposing Him to be the gardener, she said to Him, "Sir, if you have carried Him away, tell me where you have laid Him, and I will take Him away." Jesus said to her, "Mary!" She turned and said to Him in Hebrew, "Rabboni!" (which means, Teacher). Jesus said to her, "Stop clinging to Me, for I have not yet ascended to the Father; but go to My brethren and say to them, 'I ascend to My Father and your Father, and My God and your God.' " Mary Magdalene came, announcing to the disciples, "I have seen the Lord," and that He had said these things to her.

Todd Bolen/BiblePlaces.com

Todd Bolen/BiblePlaces.com

UPPER ROOM

Interesting Facts:

- *The Upper Room was where Jesus had His last supper with the Disciples.*

- *After the Resurrection the Disciples and Mary were in the Upper Room praying.*

Mark 14:12-16 On the first day of Unleavened Bread, when the Passover lamb was being sacrificed, His disciples said to Him, "Where do You want us to go and prepare for You to eat the Passover?" And He sent two of His disciples and said to them, "Go into the city, and a man will meet you carrying a pitcher of water; follow him; and wherever he enters, say to the owner of the house, 'The Teacher says, "Where is My guest room in which I may eat the Passover with My disciples?" ' "And he himself will show you a large **upper room** furnished and ready; prepare for us there." The disciples went out and came to the city, and found it just as He had told them; and they prepared the Passover.

Luke 22:10-14 And He said to them, "When you have entered the city, a man will meet you carrying a pitcher of water; follow him into the house that he enters. And you shall say to the owner of the house, 'The Teacher says to you, "Where is the guest room in which I may eat the Passover with My disciples?" ' "And he will show you a large, furnished **upper room**; prepare it there." And

Todd Bolen/BiblePlaces.com
Image on page 156 - Todd Bolen/BiblePlaces.com

they left and found everything just as He had told them; and they prepared the Passover. When the hour had come, He reclined at the table, and the apostles with Him.

Acts 1:13-14 When they had entered the city, they went up to the **upper room** where they were staying; that is, Peter and John and James and Andrew, Philip and Thomas, Bartholomew and Matthew, James the son of Alphaeus, and Simon the Zealot, and Judas the son of James. These all with one mind were continually devoting themselves to prayer, along with the women, and Mary the mother of Jesus, and with His brothers.

Todd Bolen/BiblePlaces.com

Todd Bolen/BiblePlaces.com

If you have any questions or comments, please e-mail us at:

lisalaizure@aol.com

or

robslaizure@gmail.com

Visit us at our website

www.ConnectingTheDotsMinistries.com